PENGU

BREATHE

Tania Clifton-Smith is a leading   authority on the assessment and treatment of breathing disorders, hyperventilation syndrome, physical stress management and pain syndromes. She is co-founder with Dinah Bradley Morrison of Breathing Works, the first independent breathing pattern disorders clinic in Australasia. The clinic's main focus is to treat individuals who have breathing disorders, asthma and other respiratory disorders, burnout, generalised anxiety, occupational overuse syndrome, non-specific pain syndromes, PMT and hormone imbalance disorders, fatigue and insomnia.

Tania also works as a health consultant lecturing on stress-related issues and wellness topics, assessing the workplace and individuals, and advising on implementation of wellness and health related protocols.

As a physiotherapist, Tania has worked in the private sector for four years and prior to this spent four years in the New Zealand public sector working with the pain management team co-ordinating and developing stress management and chronic pain programmes with emphasis on hyperventilation and breathing-related disorders.

Tania gained invaluable experience at the prestigious Devonshire Clinic in London where she worked for two years with eminent health professionals dealing with stress-related disorders. The clinic was targeted at business executives, entertainers and survivors of torture, all of whom are identified as a high-risk group for stress-related problems. The emphasis of treatment was on breathing re-education.

Tania presented the 'Wellness' series on Television New Zealand's 'Good Morning' show.

TESTIMONIALS

Dr Robin Kelly, GP, Auckland, who treats many patients with chronic pain disorders such as occupational overuse syndrome, chronic fatigue syndrome and fibromyalgia:
'Breathing is something everyone can do. The majority of people I see and treat are not breathing properly; I suspect the majority of the public are not breathing well either. For the chronically ill it is the first point. I believe when a person goes into a doctor's office, not only should doctors do their routine check of blood pressure, height, weight, etc, but they should also look at the breathing. To me it is the most important thing to treat.'

Dr Jan Reeves, psychiatrist:
'Many people who work long hours and have family commitments are vulnerable to developing chronic stress, with anxiety and breathing disorders. When people get nervous or anxious they tend to breathe with their upper respiratory muscles instead of their diaphragm, thus causing a breathing problem with possible hyperventilation symptoms. I routinely refer my anxious patients to Tania for treatment of any breathing problems. Her management strategies are excellent and give sufferers an effective means of helping themselves and gaining control over their breathing and anxiety.'

Dr Patrick Frengley, endocrinologist and specialist physician:
'I think it is very important for people to learn more about the physical stress reactions as well as the psychological responses. Changes occur in rates and patterns of breathing, muscle tone, pulse rate, and blood pressure, to name a few. If people have an understanding of these physical responses then they can be more effectively managed by the individual without inappropriate worry.'

Dr Margaret Wilsher, respiratory consultant:
'Hyperventilation is a common but frequently under-recognised disorder. Its sufferers often go from doctor to doctor seeking relief for a myriad of what appear to be non-specific symptoms. Once diagnosed patients are often enormously relieved to find that there is an explanation for their symptoms. The constellation of chronic fatigue, breathlessness, atypical chest pains, light-headedness and a tendency to gasp, sigh or yawn frequently should alert the clinician to the possibility that the patient is hyperventilating. Treatment should consist of physiotherapy and education about the disorder.'

Ginny, aged thirty-eight, personal assistant:
'I have been a bad sleeper all my life. Since learning to breathe well I only have the odd bad night — it's just fantastic.'

Michael, aged thirty-three, lawyer:
'You know the amazing thing is that I can now smell. I can smell my girlfriend's perfume and I can also taste food. I don't think I have experienced these sensations for at least four years. I don't know where I've been.'

Anthony, aged eight, asthmatic:
'I am not scared any more when I get short of breath. I know how to try and stop my chest tightness getting worse. I am not using my reliever as much, and I can now join in sport — that's just so neat.'

Sue, aged forty-five, teacher:
'I've got my energy back. If I feel start to feel tired, I know it is an indicator to stop, breathe and pay back the energy I have spent.'

Chris, aged twenty-eight, rower:
'Since learning to breathe through my nose, my endurance tripled within a span of three weeks — pretty easy way to train.'

Nancy, aged eighty-four:
'You told me that it was not my age causing all these nervous feelings, and you know — you were right. I can control them, I can now stop these dreadful panic attacks.'

Sally, aged fifteen, schoolgirl:
'I am not scared any more of the girls at school who have been bullying me. Before I would feel my hands tremble and go all sweaty, my throat would tighten and my heart would race. When I see them now I breathe and focus on relaxing. It makes me feel so strong and in control and then I think, who are they anyway! It also helps when I have to speak in front of the class, plus of course when I get really worried about my exams. I know it is something I have learnt that will help me in the future to cope with many things.'

Martin, aged fifty-eight, financial controller:
'This stuff actually works. If I had known about it six years ago I would not be in this physical mess now. It actually works.'

Robert, aged forty-two, barrister:
'Best thing I have learnt — my voice control in the court room is now audible, clear and strong. Before I would actually get tongue-tied at times.'

Rebecca, aged thirty-six, mother:
'I don't freeze any more at the checkout counter — a place where I used to experience a lot of my "panic attacks".'

PENGUIN BOOKS

Penguin Books (NZ) Ltd, cnr Airborne and Rosedale Roads, Albany,
Auckland 1310, New Zealand
Penguin Books Ltd, 27 Wrights Lane, London W8 5TZ, England
Penguin USA, 375 Hudson Street, New York, NY 10014, United States
Penguin Books Australia Ltd, 487 Maroondah Highway, Ringwood,
Australia 3134
Penguin Books Canada Ltd, 10 Alcorn Avenue, Toronto, Ontario,
Canada M4V 3B2
Penguin Books (South Africa) Pty Ltd, 4 Pallinghurst Road, Parktown,
Johannesburg 2193, South Africa

Penguin Books Ltd, Registered Offices: Harmondsworth, Middlesex, England

First published by Penguin Books (NZ) Ltd, 1999

3 5 7 9 10 8 6 4 2

Designed by Mary Egan
Typeset by Egan-Reid Ltd
Illustrations by Sandy Collins
Portrait photograph by Mark Cranswick
Printed in Australia by Australian Print Group, Maryborough

BREATHE TO SUCCEED

In ALL aspects of your life

TANIA CLIFTON-SMITH

PENGUIN BOOKS

CONTENTS

ACKNOWLEDGEMENTS

My thanks to colleagues who have contributed and helped me along the way: David Abercrombie, Barbara Guthrie, Rosemary Mannering, Jan Morris, Dinah Bradley Morrison and the physiotherapists at National Women's Hospital; also Dr Jim Bartley, ENT specialist; Dr Chris Ellis, cardiologist; Dr Sven Hansen; Dr Robin Kelly; Dr Ian Pogson; Dr Bill Short; Dr Rosamund Vallings; Ros Young, speech therapist; Fiona Moir from Pitch Perfect; Diana Hart, Asthma Society, Auckland; Peter Fitzsinger, sports physiologist; Grant Amos, Fear of Flying School; and Adrian Hunt at Goldfinger Secretarial Services.

Many thanks to the specialists who support my work, especially Dr Adrian Harrison, Dr Patrick Frengley and the Mercy Medical Specialist Group; Dr Margaret Honeyman, Dr Jan Reeves, Dr Peter Swinburn and Dr Margaret Wilsher. My appreciation also to the many GPs who now recognise breathing pattern disorders and refer patients for treatment.

Thanks to the team at Penguin, especially Bernice Beachman, Philippa Gerrard and Karen Brown; to Sandy Collins for the brilliant illustrations, and Mark Cranswick for the portrait photograph.

Thanks to my family and friends especially my parents who have always encouraged and supported me even when the task looked impossible; to my husband Terry for putting up with the mess of paper strewn all over the house and my absence for a few months; and to Rose for all those great meals.

Finally, my thanks to all those people who are or have been my patients, especially Ginni.

ONE

THE BODY'S
BEST-KEPT SECRET

When I began writing this book, a visiting friend said, 'How can you write about breathing? You breathe in, and then you breathe out!'

But there is so much more to breathing than 'in and out'. It is the first and the last thing we do in life. It affects our whole being — the way we feel, the way we look, the way we move, the way we function, the way we live, the way we present ourselves, and the way we speak.

Breathing affects our sleep, emotions, energy levels, performance, temperature levels and our ability to relax and to handle stress. It influences our mind, body and spirit.

A good breathing technique can assist people with asthma, poor circulation, chronic airways disease, allergies, sinusitis, headaches, high blood pressure, fatigue, and panic attacks. It can also be a great help during pregnancy and labour, lovemaking, times of stress at work or home, recovery from jet lag, substance withdrawal and pain programmes.

Breathing is the most amazing tool we have to help

us through life. It is like our best friend — always there when we need it, ready to help us through any situation, always comforting, a strength in weaker moments and a joy in calmer ones. It maintains our health and vitality, and ensures that the journey is as smooth as possible.

While breathing is something that happens automatically, it is also a function over which we have conscious control. There is nothing mystical about it, simply **'breathe well and you will be well; breathe poorly and you will be poorly'**.

Breathe to Succeed was inspired in part by increasing frustration after ten years of seeing and treating patients with breathing disorders. I now believe that many of these people could have prevented their disorders and ills given a little knowledge and a few skills. Prevention is definitely better than cure.

There is nothing more enjoyable than watching a sleeping baby. Innocence and youth are captured in the rhythmical timelessness of peaceful breathing. A parent knows when a child is unwell from the sound of his or her breathing. When the breath changes from a rhythmical, gentle pattern to a short, sharp gasping, the parent will act quickly. Parents listen at night for the sound of their child's breath, and observe the child's pattern during the day. They observe that if the mouth instead of the nose is being used to breathe, the child may be coming down with a cold; they notice when their child is short of breath because of laughter, excitement, crying or physical exhaustion. Parents are constantly assessing and diagnosing, often unaware that it is the child's breathing they are monitoring.

Many years ago, just prior to my physiotherapy finals,

I was unwittingly introduced to the power of breathing. Exam dates were looming and the pressure was on. Eating well slipped down the priority list, and exercise never occurred to me. I began to gasp for air. Being a trainee physiotherapist, I diagnosed asthma and borrowed a friend's inhaler. This gave me some relief — psychological if nothing else. However, the problem continued. I visited my GP who assured me that there was nothing wrong with me. But I felt dreadful and had exams in two weeks' time. Even worse, I was having heart palpitations and had a strange 'electric-shock' feeling, so once again I visited my GP, only to be told a second time that nothing was wrong with me.

Out of sheer frustration I persuaded a friend in the medical profession to refer me for lung function tests. Of course the tests came back negative — no asthma or lung disease but a pair of perfectly healthy lungs.

After exams I moved back home, eating healthy food regularly, working at a holiday job that involved exercise, and sleeping well — routine and balance were once again a part of my life. With time the signs and symptoms settled and my strange problem vanished.

It wasn't until 1989 that I finally understood what had been going on. At this time I was working in a prestigious London clinic which focused on business executives, actors, politicians and survivors of torture, all of whom can be exposed to an enormous amount of pressure and immense demands on the body. These people often presented with symptoms similar to my own: shortness of breath, inability to get a good breath, heart palpitations, an 'electric-shock' feeling, plus other symptoms such as chest pain, a feeling of dizziness and detachment, pins and needles to hands, mouth or legs, loss of balance, memory loss, panic attacks, anxiety, stomach problems, insomnia, and just feeling tired for no reason.

I suddenly realised what had happened to me two years earlier. I had just pushed too hard — my body had been telling me to slow down. If only I had known then what I know now — that I could use my breathing to control my body and steer it to calmer waters.

Pressure is paramount in today's society and this is only likely to increase. Those with the tools will survive; those without may not. Breathing is one of these tools.

BREATHING AND THE BOTTOM LINE

Today medical professionals and individuals look more towards prevention and wellness models than to the disease models of the past. 'Wellness' creates images of energy, positivity, vitality, endurance and happiness. Listening to the messages our body gives us — something I believe many have forgotten to do — is a powerful way to achieve this state of well-being.

The USA has encompassed this 'wellness' paradigm. The fundamental push is to encourage healthy lifestyle skills. The health of employees has become a big issue as corporations realise the effect it has on the profit and performance of the company. Aldoph Coor, founder of the Coor Corporation, has estimated that for every $1 spent on employee wellness, they have seen a return of $6.15, saving the company at least $1.9 million annually by decreasing medical costs, reducing sick leave and increasing productivity — not bad for taking a vested interest in his employees.

This trend is beginning in New Zealand with the emergence of companies such as Primary Corporate Health, a multidisciplinary medical health team whose priority is health and human performance in the workplace, while at the same time decreasing the risks of preventable diseases such as heart disease and depression.

On a smaller scale is the introduction of the 'green prescription' programme, currently in Auckland and soon to be implemented nationally. This is a wellness programme carried out by GPs in conjunction with the Hillary Commission. It has been estimated that if ten per cent of the New Zealand adult population became physically active, forty million dollars a year could be saved off the country's health bill. In the future when you visit your GP you may receive a prescription for education on the benefits of movement, activity and exercise. This drive is aimed at making our bodies stronger and more resistant to disease.

Breathing techniques have not been emphasised enough as part of this healthy lifestyle package. Many health programmes require a change in one's diet, but unless a person has a healthy system, the food will not be well processed. When we breathe well we create the optimum conditions for health and well-being; when we don't, we lay the foundation for illnesses such as heart disease, high blood pressure, digestive problems, anxiety and depression. We take our breathing for granted. Only when our breathing is impaired do we show concern. Hopefully we will soon see the introduction of 'breathing prescriptions'.

Prevention of illness is the key. But first we need awareness and education.

TWO

FINDING YOUR RHYTHM

Hippocrates, the father of modern medicine, stated some 2500 years ago that 'breathing is the basic rhythm of life'. It is important to understand the dynamics of breathing. When you understand what breathing is and what effect it has on the body you can then learn how to use the breath to your advantage.

WHAT IS A BREATH?

When discussing the breath, yogis state that 'breath is life'.

Breath has a rate, a pattern and a sound.

● The normal rate of breathing is ten to fourteen breaths per minute.

● The *pattern* at rest is rhythmical and regular.

● Air is moved in through the nose and into the lungs.

● As you breathe in your abdomen rises.

● As you breathe out your abdomen falls.

● At the end of a breath out you 'pause' before taking in a new breath.

● The *sound* is soft.

Breathing causes:

● **Movement**: This allows gas to be transported and fluid to be pumped around the body. It assists in stabilising the trunk for the upright posture and for walking and lifting.

● **Rhythm**: This has a micro-massaging effect on all the organs of the body and on the spinal column, assisting with adequate nutrition and good health.

● **Communication**: Breathing plays a major role in effective speech and voice production. It is a window into our emotional state, for example, that 'sigh' of relief, that 'gasp' of surprise, that 'groan' of pleasure.

Breathing also functions in the sense of smell. Evidence suggests that breathing connects the mind and the body.

So how do you breathe? It is time to check yourself:

In sitting position, place one hand on your chest and the other on your abdomen (stomach). Focus on your breathing — feel the pattern and the movement, and think about it for a few minutes.

● Are you breathing through your nose or your mouth?

● Which hand is moving first and most — your upper or your lower?

● How many breaths do you take in a minute (one breath equals a breath in and a breath out)?

Now think about the following and tabulate your results. Tick the appropriate column and review yourself from time to time.

Rate/min	✔		✔	Review date
Pattern		**Pattern**		

Nose
Lower hand
  moves most
Lower hand
  moves first
Pause at end
  of breath
Small breaths—
  Small volume
		Mouth
		Upper hand
		  moves most
		Upper hand
		  moves first
		No pause
		
		Large breaths—
		  Large volumes		

Rhythm		**Rhythm**		
Regular Smooth Rhythmical		Irregular Jerky Erratic		
Sound		**Sound**		
Quiet Soft Regular		Noisy Hard Stilted		

If you have a respiratory disease it may be difficult to achieve the stated rate and pattern. Pacing your breath with movement and rhythm is important for you. There is no one correct way to breathe — each of us has our own unique pattern, varying in rate, volume and rhythm. However, some breathing patterns are more effective than others and for simplicity I will talk about 'good' and 'bad' breathing patterns.

It is important to mention the volume of the air we breathe. Often this is a lot less than we might expect. Good breathing is low and slow and certainly not large in volume. It is a common misconception that deep breathing is good, but it is not necessary at rest. When you exercise or are highly stimulated, large volumes of air are required and the body chemistry changes to meet these demands. When you practise breathing exercises you will know when you are breathing deeply as you will quickly begin to feel dizzy. Deep breathing should only be used as an exercise together with certain disciplines.

Normal volumes are quite shallow. This does not mean 'upper chest' and nor does 'deep' mean 'lower chest'. 'Shallow' means a small volume of air while 'deep' means a large volume.

A 'good' pattern is:

- 10–14 breaths per minute
- Nose
- Low – abdomen
- Slow – rhythmical and small in volume

STRUCTURES THAT ENABLE US TO BREATHE

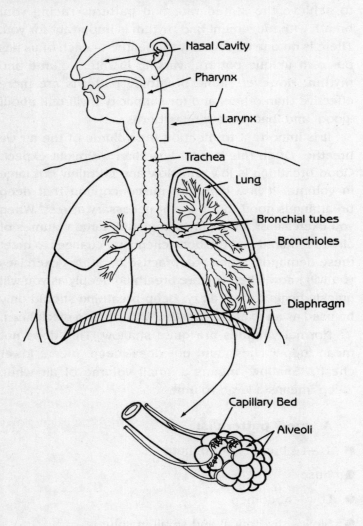

Nasal Cavity

Pharynx

Larynx

Trachea

Lung

Bronchial tubes

Bronchioles

Diaphragm

Capillary Bed

Alveoli

THE PASSAGES

The respiratory passages are made up of the nose, pharynx, larynx, trachea (windpipe) and bronchial tubes.

We breathe in through the nose, which is richly supplied with blood (this warms and humidifies the air). The air then passes through the pharynx and larynx and into the trachea. The trachea branches into two bronchi, which continue to branch into smaller and smaller bronchioles, eventually becoming the alveoli. The alveoli have very thin walls, and it is here that gas exchange occurs — oxygen is transferred through tiny tubes called capillaries into the bloodstream, where it attaches to haemoglobin in the red blood cells and is transported throughout the body. It has been estimated that in twenty-four hours approximately 20,000 litres of blood transverse the capillaries. Carbon dioxide, a by-product of this process, is transferred via the capillaries back into the airways to be expelled from the body. Inefficiencies in gas exchange will occur if the alveoli are damaged, for example, from cigarette smoking.

THE LUNGS

The lungs, which are spongy and very elastic, are divided into chambers made up of the above branching airways. They are covered in a double layer of tissue called the pleura, which is attached to the inner surface of the chest wall and the diaphragm. If the diaphragm and ribs move, so do the lungs.

THE MUSCLES

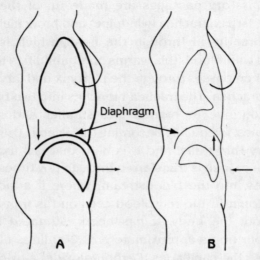

Diaphragm

A: Breathing in	B: Breathing out
The diaphragm descends inflating the lungs and compressing the abdominal contents. The abdomen and chest extends.	The diaphragm ascends deflating the lungs and releasing the abdominal contents. Abdomen and chest retract.

The diaphragm, the primary muscle of breathing, is a domed sheet composed of muscle on the outer periphery and a thick tendonous structure centrally. When we breathe in, the diaphragm descends, creating a vacuum in the upper chest cavity and causing air to be drawn into the lungs. The stomach protrudes during inhalation. The rib cage has elastic properties and as we breathe in it stretches and then recoils upon release of the diaphragm, causing air to flow out. Upon exhalation the diaphragm relaxes and the stomach flattens.

FINDING YOUR RHYTHM

The diaphragm is the only skeletal muscle that is required to function at all times. When you consider that we breathe at least 18,000 times in twenty-four hours, clearly it must be built for endurance. In times of increased demand on the body, such as when we exercise or in an emergency situation, we need to breathe harder to meet the demand. To assist with this process the muscles in the upper body start working. These muscles are known as accessory muscles of breathing. Commonly people tense these muscles and use them when it is not necessary. This quickly leads to fatigue and pain in the shoulder and neck region. Breathing with the diaphragm is the most economical and effortless way to breathe. By using the diaphragm it also normalises blood and gas flow to all the lobes of the lung.

The diaphragm separates the chest and abdominal cavities. Running through it are major vessels of the body: the vena cava, the aorta, the oesophagus and the lymphatic duct. The rhythmical movements that occur during breathing influence these vessels. It is common for people with a breathing disorder to suffer from problems such as gastric reflux — this is not surprising when you consider that the diaphragm acts like a sphincter to the oesophagus.

The heart and lungs lie above the diaphragm. The heart is encased in a tendonous sheath which merges with the central tendon of the diaphragm. Thus when we breathe the heart also moves.

The liver, stomach, intestines, spleen, kidneys, pancreas and reproductive organs lie beneath the diaphragm and also move when we breathe. The breathing movement massages these organs ensuring that they receive the oxygen and adequate nutrients they require to function in a healthy way. When a person uses upper chest breathing these organs lose this benefit and function is impaired.

The lymphatic duct travels alongside the spine at the back of the thoracic cage. Movement of this region is crucial for circulation within the lymphatic system — as this regulates our immune system it is a very important function. A good breathing pattern will move the fluid in a regular, rhythmical way. Irregular patterns may cause the fluid to stagnate, leading to health problems.

CASE HISTORIES

Sarah, aged twenty-two, suffered from tension head-aches two to three times a week since her teens. She reached the point where the headaches were severely limiting her lifestyle. It was found that Sarah was a chronic upper chest breather, using her accessory muscles as the main muscles to breathe with. These muscles were overworked and fatigued causing pain and tension.

Within six weeks Sarah had learnt to reuse her abdomen and diaphragm. Her headaches ceased totally. They return only in times of increased stress. Sarah now sees the headaches act as a good warning sign to stop and listen to her body and assess where she is at.

Kate, aged forty-two, had had constant trouble with her bowel and stomach since her teens. Her problem was that she had learnt to hold in her abdomen and this had caused bracing of the diaphragm and abdominal contents.

Kate found that when she relaxed her stomach and began to breathe abdominally, within a period of two weeks these functions had started to regulate themselves. Amazing? Not when you consider the movement that occurs in the abdominal cavity when we breathe.

❧

Jim, aged fifty-two, had had problems with gastric reflux for over a year. Within a month of breathing awareness his symptoms decreased significantly.

CONTROL OF BREATHING

The brain stem regulates breathing through a reflex activity, that is, it occurs automatically. This reflex controls the rate, depth and rhythm of breathing, and acts as a safeguard to prevent over-extension of one's capacity. For example, if we hold our breath voluntarily, eventually the reflex activity will take over, making us breathe whether we want to or not. This control occurs at an unconscious level. Even if you consciously alter the rate and depth of your breathing the reflex will kick in to regulate the volume of air inhaled. If you are a habitual bad breather, the pattern probably occurred over a period of time and slowly caused changes in the reflex setting. The sensitivity of this reflex may adapt over long periods depending on other bodily functions, for example, if respiratory disease is present or if a person has been exposed to stress over a long time.

The higher centres of the brain cortex enable you to

have conscious control of your breathing in association with the expression of emotion. For example, if you are feeling stressed and you think of a relaxed situation your breathing will change. Breathing is both a voluntary and involuntary function.

THREE

THE NOSE —
THE BODY'S SECOND-BEST
SECRET

As one patient said to me after having his nose cleared by surgery, 'Never underestimate the importance of the nose. It was not until I had to do without it that I realised what a difference it makes. In the ten days post surgery when I had to breathe with my mouth I had such a bad time. I couldn't smell, I couldn't taste food, my mouth was dry. Worst of all my sleep was disturbed and I had the most bizarre dreams — it was literally a nightmare.'

The nose performs more than a cosmetic function and goes much deeper than the protuberance on our face.

● It moistens the air.

● It warms the air.

● It filters out impurities.

This is in preparation for delivery of the air to the lower airways of the body. The nose also:

● Creates mucus, which helps protect against infection.

● Allows a sense of smell, linking the nose to experience and emotion.

● Directs airflow, which determines our physical endurance. (The inside of the nostrils of racehorses used to be clipped to make them run faster.)

● Creates pressure differences between the nose and lungs, allowing efficient gas exchange to occur. Mouth breathing results in decreased efficiency of gas exchange. Try breathing with your mouth and then with your nose. Nose breathing is similar to breathing through a straw. This increased resistance is essential to set up the correct pressure for efficient gas exchange — it actually increases the uptake of oxygen by ten to twenty per cent.

NOSE VERSUS MOUTH BREATHING

I cannot overemphasise the importance of the nose. The nose produces a gas called nitric oxide, which research suggests may have a role in

● Sterilising incoming air.

● Maintaining mucociliary clearance, preventing mucus from pooling and becoming infected.

● Functioning as a regulatory messenger in oxygen uptake and pulmonary blood flow. It is believed to be an arterial and bronchial vasodilator, playing a key role in the respiratory process ensuring good oxygenation to the body and helping to keep the airways open.

This is very exciting research. **It highlights the importance of nasal health and of breathing through the nose as a prerequisite for all health.**

If we are in the habit of breathing through the nose it is less likely to clog up. Patients often comment that the more they use their nose the better it functions. Those who suffer from allergies often find that upon starting to use the nose regularly their allergies subside.

The mouth is unable to filter impurities such as bacteria and viruses from the air we breathe, and contagious diseases may be contracted through mouth breathing. Often children who have frequent ear problems are chronic mouth breathers. If your child is predisposed to ear infections it is important to check his or her breathing pattern. Mothers in eastern countries train their babies to nose breath by tipping the head forward during sleeping — this closes the lips and makes nostril breathing imperative.

When we lie on our side, the upper nostril dilates automatically and the lower nostril closes off. This is a reflex action caused by the pressure between the arm on which we are lying and the side of the chest. For this reason many yogis recommend that when you go to bed you lie on your left side for five to ten minutes. This allows the right nostril to open, which increases the body temperature. Once you are warm and comfortable, roll on to your right side to open the left nostril. This apparently relaxes and calms you in preparation for sleep.

Throughout the night we alternate the nostril through which we breathe approximately every half hour, causing the head to move and the body to follow suit. This cycle ensures maximum rest during sleep. It has been said that the quality of sleep, the quality of breathing and the quality of life can all depend on adequate nasal function.

THE NOSE — THE BODY'S SECOND-BEST SECRET

The rhythmical alteration between nostrils occurs as a result of the swelling and shrinking of erectile tissue that lies under the outer mucosal layer lining the nose. The erectile tissue receives blood, causing the tissue to expand similarly to the erectile sexual organs. It is thought that there is a relationship between the erectile tissue in the nose and that in the breasts and sexual organs, as these are the only areas in the body that contain this tissue. A condition known as 'honeymoon nose' can occur after a period of continual sexual stimulation — the lining of the nose becomes engorged and clogged up. Perhaps there is truth in the age-old saying that you can tell how well endowed a man is by the size of his nose!

While awake, alternation between the nostrils occurs on a regular basis every one and a half to two hours. You can check this for yourself by blocking one nostril and then the other — you will find that the air will be flowing more easily through one nostril and that the more freely flowing nostril will vary throughout the day. This occurs automatically if we remain healthy and maintain a balanced lifestyle. However, factors such as emotional disturbance, poor sleep or a change in lifestyle such as skipping meals have been shown to affect this alternation. It is believed that alternating nostrils has a bearing on physical and psychological states, for example, the right nostril is thought to initiate activity and the left nostril a quieter state.

Over time, climate has affected the shape of the nose. A long, large nose is characteristic of people from cooler climates — it allows more heating of the air before it reaches the respiratory tract. Those originating from the tropics where the air is warmer and moister have wider, more open nostrils.

As a therapist I am so convinced of the importance of nose breathing that every time I see people who are mouth breathers I am tempted to approach them and beg them to start using their nose to breathe.

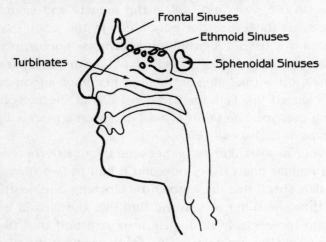

The structures that make up the nose are quite complex. The nostrils are separated by a **septum**, which allows each side to function as a separate unit. Both nostrils open into the **turbinates**, which regulate the airflow, warming and humidifying the air ready for inhalation into the body.

Mucus clears dust, grime and microbes such as viruses and bacteria out of the air. It has been estimated that we inhale around twenty billion particles of foreign matter a day so it is importance to keep the mucus flowing — if it pools for too long it can rapidly become infected.

THE NOSE — THE BODY'S SECOND-BEST SECRET

Cilia are hair-like structures that are responsible for clearing mucus away. If the mucus becomes too thick or thin the cilia become ineffective. The main determinant of the consistency of our mucus is food — it is well known that milk products, for example, create thicker and more viscous mucus.

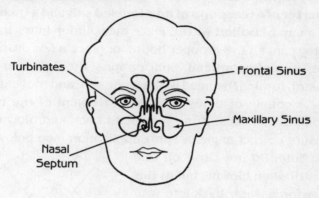

Small passages from the sinuses lead into the nasal cavity, allowing for the removal of mucus. These passages can easily become blocked, creating pressure, which may result in a sinus headache. Because of the shape of our maxillary sinuses mucus can become stagnant and lead to sinusitis (infection of the sinuses).

Several things will help to maintain nasal health.

NASAL WASHES

Nasal washes are a common practice in Asia and eastern countries.

Salt water is a natural wash for the linings of the nasal cavity as it is similar to the composition of tears, which are salty and drain into the nose along the sinuses. It is well known that people who regularly swim in the sea have excellent nasal health. In eastern religious practice it is not uncommon to clear the sinuses with a wash using a neti pot prior to meditation. (A neti pot may be purchased from Asian stores.)

A **nasal wash** can be made by mixing together **a quarter of a teaspoon of non-iodised salt** and **a quarter of a cup of boiled water**. Place the solution into a nasal spray can, an eye dropper bottle, or place a few drops in the palm of your hand. Sniff or spray the fluid into the nostril, turning the head to the same side and moving the jaw a couple of times to allow movement of the fluid along the sinuses. Bring your head back and blow out. Ensure correct angle of spray application (see below).

Note: Do not close off one nostril when blowing out as this may force water back into your ear. If the water enters the upper sinuses you may experience an uncomfortable stinging sensation. This will not harm you so don't be deterred, as healthy, clear nasal passages are extremely important.

A nasal wash can be used three times a week for health maintenance or, if you have a nasal infection, twice a day until the infection improves. This rinse can also be used as a mouth gargle if you have a sore

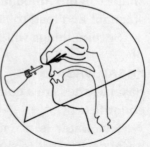

throat or as a general cleanser for the mouth and throat.

STEAM INHALATION

If you have a nasal infection, a steam inhalation can be used twice a day for two weeks. Place boiling water in a pot or bowl, drape the head with a towel and lean over the water to inhale the steam. Friar's balsam can be added to the water if you wish. Take care not to burn yourself.

HEAD POSITIONING FOR NASAL DRAINAGE

Lying flat, turn your head forty-five degrees on your pillow. Remain in this position for up to ten minutes then change sides. This positioning allows drainage of the maxillary sinuses.

TRACTION

At times pressure can build up in the sinuses and lead to a sinus headache. Traction of the small bones that form the sinuses is a most effective way to relieve this pressure. Place fingers on the areas highlighted with x — then gently place pressure in the direction of the arrows. Hold for 20–30 seconds and repeat three times.

PRESSURE POINTS

Placing pressure on the lower surface of your clavicle (collar bone) where it joins the sternum (breast bone) can help to decrease nasal obstruction and assist with lymphatic movement. Gently press upwards in this region as if to lift the collar bone. Hold for the count of ten.

Pressure placed on the uppermost rib (hold the area and pull downwards) assists with the release of air out the nose. This is an excellent exercise if you are prone to breathing large volumes of air.

BACK MOBILITY

Mobility in the region of the mid back is important for adequate nasal functioning. The stretches on pages 72–75 will be helpful.

Try the following: In sitting position breathe through the nose in a relaxed way, feeling the rhythmical pattern. Now tense hard between the shoulderblades and notice what happens to your breathing pattern. You will probably find that it is difficult to use your nose.

CASE HISTORY

Andy, aged thirty-eight, had a history of years of suffering from digestive problems. He had constant nausea with episodes of severe diarrhoea and abdominal pain. He often took antibiotics.

Andy played a lot of sport, especially rugby, and had injured himself on several occasions, twice breaking his nose. Further questioning revealed that Andy often suffered from muscular aches and pains to his neck and shoulders, and from headaches which he knew came on with increased tension.

The first thing I noticed was that Andy was a chronic mouth breather. This predisposed him to breathing into his upper chest, therefore using his neck and shoulder muscles to breathe. This instantly explained the muscular pains and headaches. (The upper body muscles should only be used for breathing when we are under stress, such as when running.)

Mouth breathers' systems are required to work harder, making larger demands on the body and weakening the system. In Andy's case it did not help his digestive problems. Andy had no structural damage of any significance to his nose. Within four weeks, nose breathing had become almost automatic and his neck and shoulder pain disappeared. His nausea and digestive problems lessened by fifty per cent within four weeks and now, six months later, he hardly has any problems. However, to quote Andy, 'When the nausea returns I realise that I have been overdoing things and breathing incorrectly. All I do is concentrate on relaxed breathing for a day or so and it subsides.'

It has been said that man should no more breathe through his mouth than he would attempt to take food through his nose.

FOUR

UNDERSTANDING
YOUR BODY

Breathing has three main functions:

1   When we breathe in we **take in oxygen**, which travels through the nasal passages to the lungs to enter the bloodstream. Oxygen is necessary for the body to convert food into energy in order to 'power' the body and enable all cells to function.

2   When we exhale we **breathe out carbon dioxide**, the end result of this metabolism.

3   Breathing **preserves the acid-alkaline balance (pH)**. This is the balance between the amount of carbonic acid and bicarbonate in the blood; this must be kept at a constant value of 7.4.

Breathing has an inverse relationship with energy. The rate, rhythm, depth and flow of our breaths will determine the quality and quantity of the energy we receive. For example, if our breathing rate speeds up, so does the amount of energy we use. When we sprint, for example, our breathing is fast, explosive and peaked and our energy output is high. When we are tense and

UNDERSTANDING YOUR BODY

breathe into our upper chest the breath is faster, larger and sharper, and more energy is used. **Large volumes** are more demanding of muscular work, and also **use up more energy**.

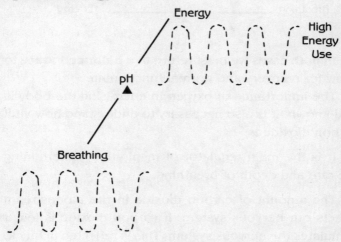

If our breathing rate slows down, so does the amount of energy we use. The breathing of long-distance runners is easier, less peaked and more regulated than

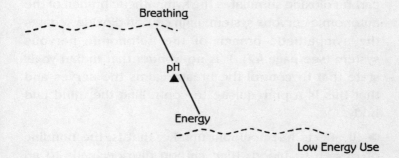

sprinters — this enables endurance as energy consumption is lower. When we are **relaxed** our **breathing** is rhythmical and slow and **energy consumption is low**.

Breathing ——————— pH ——————— Energy

In both cases we must return to a **balanced state** to allow for recovery and normal functioning.

The importance of oxygen in energising the body is well known. It is also necessary to understand how vital carbon dioxide is:

● It is the main regulator of respiration, determining the rate and depth of breathing.

● The amount of carbon dioxide in the bloodstream affects our nervous system. If carbon dioxide is low it stimulates the nervous system. This is reflected in quick, erratic breathing. A high level of carbon dioxide sedates the nervous system resulting in relaxed, rhythmical breathing.

● It regulates the activity of the autonomic nervous system, which controls the organs of the body. Low carbon dioxide stimulates the sympathetic branch of the autonomic nervous system; high carbon dioxide sedates the sympathetic branch of the autonomic nervous system (see page 47). It is no wonder that Indian yogis state that to control the breath calms the nerves and that this is a prerequisite to controlling the mind and body.

● It affects haemoglobin uptake, that is, the bonding of oxygen to blood. High carbon dioxide leads to an increase of oxygen to the cells; low carbon dioxide decreases the oxygen uptake and compromises the amount of energy available to the cells.

● It affects coronary and carotid artery constriction (coronary arteries supply blood to the heart; carotid arteries supply blood to the brain). If carbon dioxide is low the vessels become constricted. This can cause coronary arterial spasm, which can simulate a heart attack. Carotid artery constriction causing decreased blood to the brain can cause symptoms such as fogginess, poor memory and dizziness. High carbon dioxide has a dilatory effect on the vessels.

● Carbon dioxide maintains the acid/alkaline balance. It forms the carbonic acid buffer, which is important in the removal of waste products of energy production such as lactic acid from the muscles. If this buffer becomes depleted there is a rapid build-up of lactic acid in the muscles. This is why performing an activity for too long without a rest can result in sore, aching muscles.

Left to itself our breathing centre will maintain and regulate our breathing — the goal is to maintain normal blood levels of carbon dioxide, thus maintaining the pH. However, certain factors alter this balance.

The rate and depth of breathing can cause carbon dioxide levels to fluctuate. Low, slow breathing can lead to drowsiness and is valuable in assisting us with sleep. A rapid, sharp inhalation followed immediately by an exhalation will cause a drop in carbon dioxide and if this is prolonged it stimulates the body, for example,

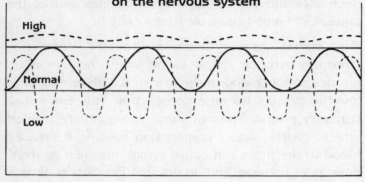

Arterial blood levels of CO_2 and the effect on the nervous system

High

Normal

Low

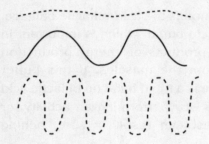

Low Volume/Slower
Sedates nervous system

Balance at rest

Large Volume/Faster
Stimulates nervous system

when we over-breathe at rest, run or speak rapidly without pausing for breath.

Certain disorders cause alterations in carbon dioxide levels. The table on page 45 shows factors that can cause a drop in carbon dioxide. As a result breathing will change to accommodate this drop. If low levels of carbon dioxide are maintained a breathing disorder known as hyperventilation syndrome may develop. This is a breathing disorder characterised by over-breathing at rest.

ETIOLOGICAL FACTORS IN BREATHING PATTERN DISORDERS

Lung Disease
Asthma, bronchitis, emphysema

Physiological Changes
Temperature, altitude, humidity, talking

Anaemia

Drugs
Caffeine, nicotine, aspirin, amphetamines, cocaine, crack, ecstasy

Posture
Slouched, rigid, bracing posture seen in post cardiac, respiratory or abdominal surgery, or with vanity (holding in the stomach, wearing high heels, tight clothes, corsets, belts, etc)

Psychiatric
Anxiety, panic, depression

Metabolic
Diabetes, liver failure, renal failure

Endocrine
Pregnancy, alteration in progesterone levels

Pain

Occupation Related
Singers, divers, swimmers, wind instrument players, military personnel, ballerinas, computer workers

Speech
Rapid, breathless talkers

Mouth Breathing
Nasal obstruction, glasses blocking nose

Sustaining Factors

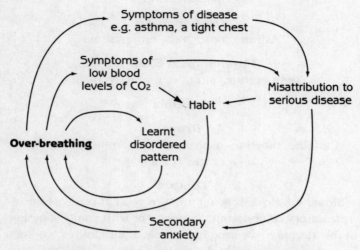

(Adapted from William Gardner, 'The Pathophysiology of
Hyperventilation Disorder', reprinted with permission.)

Note that all the above can cause altered breathing
patterns. However, not all breathing disorders or poor
breathing patterns result in hyperventilation. What
commonly occurs is that once the cause or initiating
factor is corrected or removed a bad breathing pattern
remains, this in itself causing a host of new problems. It
is useful to try to establish the initiating factor to give an
indication of the length of time the bad pattern has been
in place.

When checking the history of patients they often reveal
that they have suffered from asthma or have had bronchitis
or pneumonia within the last six months. Alternatively,
they may have undergone an intensely stressful period a
year or so ago, or they may simply have been instructed

as a child to hold the stomach in. If a bad breathing pattern has been established, a conscious effort must be made to revert back to a good one.

If you are worried that you have a bad breathing pattern and are unsure about the reason, visit your GP to rule out anything sinister and then focus on correcting your breathing pattern.

Involuntary hypoventilation (under-breathing) can only be induced for brief periods. As the carbon dioxide builds up it stimulates the respiratory centre to override voluntary breathing and assume involuntary control.

Hypoventilation can be caused by:

1 Drugs, for example, analgesics or barbiturates — these have a sedating effect on the metabolic system causing a decreased drive in breathing. They may be given to people who are hyperventilating because of over-anxiety or pain to help restore breathing to normal.

2 Hypoxia (decreased oxygen to the brain). This will decrease the respiratory drive, increasing blood levels of carbon dioxide. Very high levels can cause acute respiratory failure, which is potentially life-threatening.

3 Damage to the nerves supplying the muscles of breathing caused by trauma or diseases such as motor neuron disease.

THE AUTONOMIC NERVOUS SYSTEM

The autonomic nervous system controls the organs of the body and plays a crucial role in stress-related disorders. One of the first things we do in response to a

Autonomic Nervous System	
Sympathetic	Parasympathetic
Papillary dilation	Papillary constriction
↓ Salivation	↑ Salivation
↑ Muscle tension	↓ Muscle tension
↑ Breathing rate	↓ Breathing rate
↑ Heart rate	↓ Heart rate
↑ Blood pressure	↓ Blood pressure
Release of glucose by liver	Stimulation of gallbladder
↓ Digestion	↑ Digestion
Bladder contraction	Bladder relaxation
Genital inhibition	Genital stimulation
↑ Perspiration	↓ Perspiration

stressful situation is to alter our breathing.

The autonomic nervous system consists of two parts: the sympathetic and the parasympathetic. The sympathetic branch acts in a 'fight or flight' manner, readying the body for action. The senses become alert, the mouth dry, the eyes sensitive to light, and the heart rate increases to pump more blood to the muscles that have contracted ready for action. The airways open and breathing speeds up to carry oxygen to the muscles. There is decreased sexual drive and the digestive system shuts down so that blood can be redirected to the muscles. Increased demand on the body increases the release of stress hormones.

This response normally occurs when we get excited or nervous, for example, when we speak publicly or are in a stressful situation such as a car accident. If no physical activity occurs or the situation is prolonged and the body is not allowed to recover, the sympathetic branch can remain switched on causing breathing patterns to alter and, over time, exhaustion and ill health to occur.

The parasympathetic branch of the nervous system has a much more sedentary role and functions while the body is at rest. It regulates all phases of digestion and controls resting activities. It is important to spend time in both of these states for balance to occur.

Breathing can stimulate both the sympathetic and the parasympathetic nervous system. When you feel nervous, for example, the sympathetic branch is stimulated causing symptoms such as sweaty palms, a tight chest and a racing heart. If you focus on your breathing, regulating it to a low, slow rhythmical pattern as soon as you begin to feel anxious, you can activate the parasympathetic branch and dampen your anxiety. It is not uncommon to see performers backstage relaxing themselves with breathing techniques.

Just as you can relax yourself with your breathing, you can also stimulate yourself. An artist friend will often breathe rapidly prior to beginning to paint in order to stimulate the sympathetic nervous system and let the creative juices flow.

Let's learn to use this ability to our advantage!

FIVE

LEARN TO BREATHE

There are three basic types of breathing: relaxed, effective and stimulatory. These are used to enhance relaxation, health and performance.

By now you should be aware of your breathing pattern — if not, follow the simple exercise on page 17.

RELAXED BREATHING

This is what I call pure belly (stomach) breathing — it is breathing in its simplest form. As you breathe in, the diaphragm descends causing the stomach to protrude. As you breathe out, the diaphragm ascends and the stomach flattens.

1   In sitting position place one hand on your chest and the other on your abdomen. Focus on your breathing. Feel the pattern and the movement and think about it for a few minutes.

2   **Breathe** all the air **out** through your nose or mouth and then relax.

3   Now gently **breathe in** through your nose and think

about letting your stomach rise as the air comes into your lower hand.

4   Feel your stomach and your lower hand drop as you **breathe out** through your nose.

5   Try a gentle **pause** after exhaling.

6   If you find this difficult try breathing in a little lower to the bottom of your lungs, applying a firmer pressure with your lower hand to increase the resistance. The next breath will draw air into the bottom of your lungs.

7   Continue with this pattern, aiming for a smooth, regular rhythm, for five to ten minutes.

Remember: *Nose/low/slow and let go.*

Visualising and associating the movement of the air may help. Try imagining the breath as a circle, a wave or a swinging pendulum.

Note that you may experience 'air hunger', which is a feeling of having to take a deeper breath. This is common and indicates that you are not used to the low, slow pattern or that you are trying too hard. When you experience air hunger, swallowing will help to decrease the sensation. With time the feeling will lessen — it often eases after one week of practice. If your breathing has been 'bad' for some time, it may take longer to change to a more regulated pattern.

I discourage counting during this exercise as it tends to lead to over-controlled breathing. However, initially it may be helpful to establish your rhythm. For example, breathe in, one, two (two seconds) . . . and out, one, two, three (three seconds) . . . and pause. Try using words instead of numbers, for example, 'breathe in . . . and let go . . .; breathe in . . . and relax . . . '

Exhaling should take longer than inhaling. A longer breath out causes mental and physical relaxation at rest.

The pause after exhaling is also important. The pause phase stills the mind. You may feel that you are doing nothing but air is actually still being exhaled. Most of us don't exhale for long enough; this is a common problem with people who suffer from asthma. The longer the pause, the more relaxing the breath and the more relaxed you will feel. When practising allow the pause to be as long as you want. Play with it — don't worry if you extend it for a long time as the breath in will come again.

Try taking a breath in and out with a pause, and then try without a pause. Do you notice a difference? If you are not accustomed to relaxed breathing you will initially notice that it may be difficult to pause. As you become more used to it the pause will become easier and longer in duration.

In relaxed breathing the aim is to move air in and out without effort, increasing both the time taken to exhale and the pause time between breaths. **Mastery is attained when you can breathe in a low, slow, rhythmical pattern with a longer breath out than in, and where the pause is sustainable without air hunger.** This pattern leads to internal relaxation, inner calm, a stilled mind and peripheral warming. It is ideal prior to sleep, in stressful situations, and for regeneration of energy. This is the preferable pattern at rest.

Practising in front of a mirror can be helpful. Do it

whenever you can find time to allow yourself to 'catch up'.

To begin with the pattern may feel strange. To quote Denise, aged twenty-two: *'The first time I tried relaxed breathing I did not like it — it felt so foreign — but as I got used to it I welcomed the relaxation it gave me. I now use it daily.'*

LONGER RELAXATION BREATHING

I recommend using the following exercise twice a day for ten to fifteen minutes:

1   Lie on the floor or on the bed and allow your legs to drop outwards. You may wish to place a pillow under your legs. Place your arms at your sides so that they are not touching your body and turn your palms upwards. Close your eyes.

2   Scan your body for tension, especially your throat, tongue, jaw, chest and abdomen. Often when we are nervous or have an altered breathing pattern for some reason we tend to breathe a short, shallow breath into our upper chest. That is why it is important to release all physical tension before you start:

● Stretch, pulling your toes back towards your shins and then allowing them to drop.

● Roll your knees out to each side and let them drop.

- Tense your thighs and buttocks and then let them drop.

- Pull your shoulders to your ears and then let go.

- Stretch your fingers and your thumbs and then let them drop.

- Gently pull your chin in towards the pillow and then relax.

- Raise your eyebrows to your forehead and then let them drop.

- Check that your jaw and tongue are loose inside your mouth.

3 Now think about your breathing — low and slow through the nose. Check your body again for any tension — repeat the sequence above if any remains.

4 Rest your tongue on the roof of your mouth. Place both your hands gently on your stomach and chest and follow your breathing. Breathing in through your nose, allow your stomach to rise gently. Breathe in as much as you feel is comfortable. Let the air fall out, relaxing your whole body as you breathe out. Feel the stomach and chest drop. Think, 'Let go.'

   If you find this difficult try adding a little pressure on your stomach using your hand, a box of tissues or a book — this will increase your awareness of where to breathe and will help to strengthen the diaphragm.

5 Think about the rise and fall of your breath as you inhale and exhale. Note how your abdomen rises with each inhalation and falls with each exhalation; notice the pause before you breathe in again.

6 Let your chest follow the movement of your abdomen. Focus on the sound and feel of your breathing as you become more and more relaxed. Ensure that your breath out is longer than your breath in.

7 At the end of each breathing session take a little time to check your body again for tension. Compare the tension you feel at the end of your exercise with that when you began. When you become easier with your breathing, relax and think about the low, slow rhythm.

If it is difficult to breathe through your nose, clear your nasal passages before doing the breathing exercises. (See the nasal wash on page 34.)

Relaxation creates a floating, calm, warm feeling. For those of you who have not felt this before — enjoy it. You may find it useful if initially a friend or your partner reads the relaxation out, or you may wish to make yourself a tape.

When you've learnt to relax using relaxed breathing, practise it whenever you feel tense — while sitting, standing or moving. Generally it takes six to eight weeks to introduce new patterns of movement and breathing to the body. Like anything, it takes time and practice.

BREATHING FOR MEDITATION
Meditation means the act of reflecting, contemplating spiritual matters, achieving inner calm and stilling of the mind. In eastern cultures the spirit and breath are closely linked. 'Inspiration' means 'in spirit'. It is believed that spirit is breath and that when you stop

breathing your spirit dies or leaves you, as does your breath. When talking about spiritual issues the breath is often a focal point.

There are many different types of meditation. One of the most basic forms is to relax and focus on your breathing, to feel the rhythm of the breath in and the breath out, and to pause and think of the flow. (In effect you are doing your relaxed breathing exercise.)

If you wish to try meditating, stand, sit or lie in a comfortable position where you will not be distracted. Now think about your breathing. Think about the inhalation and the exhalation. Mentally start counting the breath in: one, two, three, four, five, six . . . and out: one, two, three, four, five, six, seven . . . pause. If you find this count too deep, try in: one, two, three . . . and out: one, two, three, four . . . pause. Your breathing should be a little slower than during rest, which is generally in: one, two . . . and out: one, two, three . . . pause. If nothing else you will realise how difficult it is to still the mind! Try to meditate for about ten minutes.

POSTURE

It is important here to mention posture. When we look at breathing in the upright position, efficient body posture must be implemented.

The increase in sedentary lifestyles has led to poor postures, for example, slouching, tight, caved-in upper chests and stooped shoulders, and with this comes poor breathing patterns. Efficient body posture is when the body is in good alignment.

a) **Good alignment.**

1 Chin gently tucked in.

2 Neck in a straight line with the shoulders parallel to the floor.

3 Shoulders relaxed, gently pulled backwards and with the shoulderblades down.

4 Abdomen taut. Diaphragm relaxed.

5 Pelvis gently tucked in with the bottom of your hips in line with the centres of your feet.

6 Knees relaxed.

7 Feet standing shoulder-width apart.

Stand as if you have a piece of string coming out of the top of your head. Now imagine that I am pulling the string and your body is correcting its alignment as above. Finally, gently breathe out and relax the frame around your new found alignment.

Two opposites of this posture are:

b) **Slouched posture.** The body tends to cave in and there is no resistance provided in the abdominal cavity, so that breathing is inefficient. The centre of gravity is usually displaced into the upper chest.

c) **Rigid posture.** Restricted posture, with little movement and a lot of physical tension held in the musculature. A tense back and abdomen works like a corset — it is well known that wearing a corset is extremely bad for your breathing. Imagine the poor ladies of the nineteenth century, fainting because of air hunger and relying on smelling salts and the perpetual movement of air from their fans to keep them going. This posture also displaces the centre of gravity upwards.

If the body is in good alignment, less energy is required to breathe and move, and there is optimum resistance for the diaphragm to work against. The Alexander Technique advocates that good posture is a prerequisite to efficient breathing — this is correct in part but it can also work in reverse.

Research is currently looking at the use of all abdominal muscles in movement. Emerging work shows that the stabilisers to the trunk region (the transversus abdominus and the internal oblique) work in conjunction with the diaphragm, the pelvic floor muscles and the back muscles. This makes sense as these muscles form a box-type compartment in our trunk region. What researchers have noticed is that if we breathe incorrectly the firing of these muscles is altered, suggesting that 'good' breathing is a prerequisite to optimum body movement.

EFFECTIVE BREATHING

Once you have mastered relaxed breathing, the next progression is effective breathing. This should occur in normal day-to-day activity.

1 A good posture is necessary. If sitting, ensure your bottom is back in the chair and your chest is open and relaxed. If standing, make sure your feet are hip-width apart with your pelvis in line, chest open and head up.

2 Placing your hands on your lower rib cage with your fingers towards your stomach, breathe in so that your hands move out and sideways.

3 Breathing in through your nose, inhale steadily, allowing the abdomen to rise gently and the lower ribs to move sideways. You will notice that the chest also moves gently. Now exhale. This sideways movement is essential as it places increased tension on the abdominal muscles and fascia creating an increase in tension of the abdomen. This allows efficient movement and strength of the diaphragm, giving increased efficiency in breathing and gas exchange.

This breathing pattern also ensures total trunk strength and stability. It is of utmost importance for those involved in jobs which require lifting. For a full exhalation after you have breathed out, gently tighten and draw in the stomach, forcing out the remaining air. This needs to be done only occasionally and is not a part of regular practice.

EFFECTIVE BREATHING EXERCISE

This exercise is to be done as a
series of full, complete breaths
several times a day. It uses
all the respiratory muscles.
Do not force the exercise.

1   Place your hands on your
    abdomen and the side of
    your chest and feel a
    relaxed breath.

2   Place your hands on the sides
    of your body and feel the breath move towards the
    lower ribs.

3   Place one hand on your upper chest and feel the air
    enter it.

4   Work to merge these steps into a continuous breath.

QUICK FIX FOR 'INSTANT CALM'

When there are too many files open in a computer you
run the risk of it shutting down — the brain also works
like this. The following exercise enables you to close
down files. It is useful in peak-hour traffic, when dealing
with rude customers, or when things have just become
too much.

1   Stop.

2   Breathe out.

3   Pause and relax.

4   Breathe in through the nose with a low, slow breath.

5   Breathe out for as long as you can, releasing all

muscle tension as you do.

6   Pause — still your mind and your body.

7   Continue what you were previously doing.

Note: It is a good idea to inform others that you are working on re-training your breathing. Family and friends can give little reminders such as a nudge in the ribs if you are breath holding, or remind you to slow your speech or breathe slowly through the nose.

STIMULATORY BREATHING

a.   Cleansing the lungs and removing stale air

1   In sitting or standing position, breathe in through your nose.

2   Purse your lips as if to whistle and then blow out.

3   Ensure that all the air is expelled — blow out in several short, sharp breaths and then finally one long one.

4   Inhale sharply into the back of the nose.

5   Gently release the breath.

b.   Stimulation

1   Sitting in a relaxed position check that the tip of your tongue is resting on the gum just above your upper front teeth — keep it there throughout the exercise.

2   Breathe in rapidly through your nose.

3   Breathe out just as rapidly through your nose. If you place your hand on your stomach you should feel your diaphragm working in forceful breaths. You

should be able to hear the breath. Do approximately three breaths per second then try ten breaths.

4   Resume normal breathing.

This is a way of activating the nervous system. As you feel more comfortable you can build up the time to about thirty seconds. Stimulating breathing used in conjunction with movement is an excellent pick-me-up instead of a cup of coffee.

Note: If you feel 'spaced out' you may have been hyper-ventilating into the upper chest instead of using the force of the diaphragm.

INSTANT ENERGISING BREATHING STRETCHES
These stretches will increase the blood flow and re-energise the brain.

a.

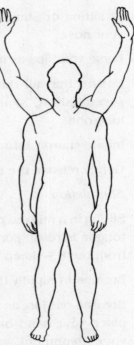

1   Standing with your feet shoulder-width apart, tail tuck (tilt your pelvis backwards, knees slightly bent).

2   Lift both arms above your head and interlock your fingers, stretching up as you breathe in through the nose. Hold for a second.

3 Let your arms drop down to your sides and breathe out through the nose.

4 Repeat three times.

b.

1 Standing with your feet shoulder-width apart, tail tuck and inhale, stretching your arms and shoulderblades forward at shoulder height.

2 Exhale and stretch your arms, pulling your shoulderblades together behind your back.

GUIDE TO BREATHING RE-EDUCATION

Week 1: Breathing awareness — learn to use the nose again. Using the **green dot method**, strategically place your green dots on the fridge or telephone, for example, to work as a feedback tool to remind you to nose breathe using low, slow breaths, on average three to four times an hour. Stop when you see the dot — breathe out and find that calm feeling. Then continue what you were previously doing.

Week 2: Longer relaxation breathing twice a day, essential prior to sleep. Use the **green dot**

method to remind you to use relaxation breathing when you feel nervous or angry. Begin upper body stretches, see pages 71–75.

Week 3: Identify triggers, practise when you feel nervous, angry or low in mood.

Week 4: Strengthen the diaphragm. Add a weight to your relaxation sessions, ie, place an iron or a weight on your stomach and use this to increase resistance. Start with 3 x 30 seconds and progress to 3 x 2 minutes.

Week 5: Continue with the above exercises.

Week 6: Stimulatory breathing exercises and stretches, see pages 63–65.

It is important to realise that it is unhealthy to focus on your breathing all the time as this can also lead to problems. Remember that breathing out is a passive movement, that is, no control is required — the diaphragm just relaxes. Continue with awareness, and practice for as long as it takes for the correct breathing pattern to become an automatic reaction.

BREATHING WITH EXERCISE

Breathing patterns should be matched to the activity or task. As an activity speeds up, our breathing pattern changes. A sprinter, for example, requires an increased volume of air and will have an increased rate of breathing and no pause time between breaths. When walking, the breathing rate is less, less air is moved, and the pause time is longer. Problems occur when there is a mismatch, such as breathing as if you are sprinting when you are walking.

If you move in a relaxed, graceful manner you will begin to feel this way. Imagine you need to ask directions in a busy street. I am sure you would feel more comfortable approaching someone who is walking in a relaxed manner rather than someone who is walking with a sharp, tense stride — this often reflects how the person feels. Think of the difference between the walking style of a Jamaican and an upper-class Englishman. The walking rhythm will often reflect the breathing pattern.

The rhythm of the feet provides a regular beat with which to co-ordinate your breathing. Walking at a normal pace, try taking two steps for a breath in, two for a breath out, then pause. Start the activity breathing with your nose in and out, and continue for as long as possible as this will increase your endurance. As the activity increases in difficulty start using the nose to breathe in and the mouth to breathe out. As the pace gets harder you can use your mouth to breathe in and out of, but ensure that your breathing is regular, for example, breathe in counting one, two . . . and out, one, two, three, or in, one . . . and out, one, two. Finally, on that steep hill, count in, one . . . out, one. Aim to co-ordinate your breathing and movement using a regular rhythm and a longer exhalation than inhalation. The golden rule is never to pant.

CAUTION

When practising the breathing patterns described above, it is possible that you may experience any of the following:

● Light headedness — this is due to over-breathing, that is, taking too large a volume of air.

● Giddiness upon standing — this is due to over-breathing or moving too rapidly after relaxing.

● Strong emotions — this can happen if you have been very tense because of a past trauma or experience and then begin to let go. Allow yourself to relax gradually and the sensation will pass.

Should you experience any of the above just relax and settle into your normal breathing pattern.

Note that the breathing guidelines given relate to 'normal' values. However, your breathing is unique. If you feel you require assistance your GP will be able to refer you to a skilled physiotherapist.

COMMON BREATHING PROBLEMS THAT MAY LEAD TO A DISORDERED PATTERN

● Mismatch in breathing pattern and activity, eg, overbreathing at rest.

● Breath holding — this is common with certain tasks, for example, bending to tie a shoelace, working at a computer, standing, concentrating, stretching or when fearful.

● Irregular size of breaths — too large or too shallow.

● Frequent yawning or sighing. It is normal to take a deep breath several times within an hour but it is not normal to take deep, sighing breaths in succession. If you find yourself doing this, try to suppress the sigh or yawn by swallowing — this will break the cycle.

● Sniffing, coughing or frequent throat clearance.

● Fast, breathless talking.

● General body tension.

DISORDERED BREATHING PATTERNS

Most of us experience an altered breathing pattern at some stage, but for some the pattern becomes engrained and our bodies alter accordingly. Disordered breathing patterns are an indication that we are not well or are running inefficiently.

Upper chest breathing with large inflated breaths: This pattern commonly appears in people who have learned to hold in their abdomen, often because of fashion or the desire to be thin. It is well known that many models suffer from panic attacks and episodes of fainting. This is not surprising when you see how contracted and restricted their diaphragms are, thus causing the breathing to be totally upper chest and leading to chronic hyperventilation.

Forget everything you were ever taught about holding the stomach in. This can be difficult, especially for older women who grew up in the corset era. One patient told me she found letting go of her abdomen 'quite liberating'.

Upper chest, thoracic breathing: This results in less efficient gas exchange and is often associated with increased anxiety. It may occur following surgery or bracing (tightening) of the diaphragm or as a result of fashion.

Rapid, regular, upper chest breathing: This is observed in patients with pulmonary disease and in children with adenoid hypertrophy. It can also be seen when someone is starting to 'wind up'.

Rapid, irregular, upper chest breathing: This is often associated with emotional disturbance, anxiety and panic.

Low rate, regular pattern: A breathing rate of less than eight breaths per minute can often be seen in Caucasians with nasal injuries. The injury can increase the nasal resistance, which slows down the rate.

Low rate, irregular pattern: This is commonly seen in people with chronic fatigue, exhaustion and depression.

Rigid or statue breathing: The breathing is extremely shallow with short, sharp inspirations and expirations, and the body appears not to move at all. I have noticed this pattern with patients who have been exposed to fear or anxiety over a long period of time. This pattern can take a long time to alter as the person slowly learns to let go of physical and emotional tension.

Cogwheel breathing: The breathing becomes more and more inflated to the point where you feel you can no longer breathe in — in fact what is required is a breath out.

Paradoxical breathing: Reverse breathing pattern occurs. This is commonly found in individuals with severe lung disease.

BREATHING SOUNDS
Different sounds can have different meanings.

LEARN TO BREATHE

● Rapid speech with gasps in through the mouth as a few more words are squeezed out can be indicative of a braced diaphragm and upper chest breathing.

● Quiet speech that fades may point to diaphragm weakness. Often a slouched, caving-in posture is seen.

● Throat clearing — this can indicate nervousness and anxiety.

● Snorting may be a result of sheer exhaustion.

● Long sighs and yawning are indicative of fatigue and exhaustion.

Many factors can alter our breathing pattern (see the chart on page 45). Tension and loss of body awareness are the most common reasons.

Try the following exercise: In sitting position place your hand on your stomach at the bottom of your breastbone (sternum). Feel your breathing in and out then quickly clench your other fist and feel what happens to the diaphragm. The instant a threat is posed our diaphragm contracts. Try clenching your jaw or tensing your thigh or pelvis and think about the way the diaphragm reacts. This contraction in turn alters the body chemistry — adrenaline starts pumping and we are alerted and readied for action. A problem arises when there is no action.

STRETCHES FOR THE UPPER CHEST
These stretches are especially important if you have had a bad breathing pattern for a long period of time.

ROTATIONS

1 Standing two feet out from the wall, feet shoulder-width apart, tail tuck (see page 125), inhale and rotate the body around so that both your hands can touch the wall.

2 Exhale and return to the mid-line.

3 Repeat three times in both directions.

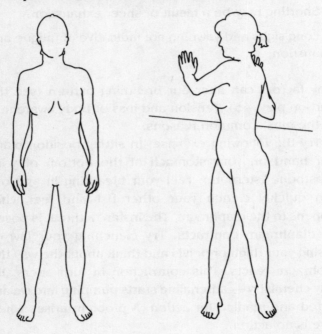

MID CHEST STRETCH

1   Interlace your fingers, then straighten your arms in front of you, breathe in and stretch forwards.

2   Interlace fingers behind your back breathe out and stretch backwards and upwards.

3   Repeat three times.

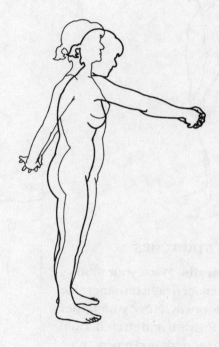

SHOULDER ROLLS BACKWARDS

Roll your shoulders, shoulderblades and upper chest backwards stretching as far back as possible. Do a complete circle. Repeat three times.

MUSCLE STRETCHES

1 **Pectoralis**. Place your elbows at shoulder height on either side of a doorway. Move your upper body forward and stretch. Hold for 10 seconds and repeat three times. You may wish to move your arms higher then lower to stretch different areas of the pectoralis muscle in the front chest wall.

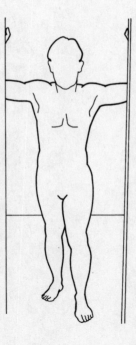

2   **Upper trapezius**. Place one arm behind your back.
     Gently tilt your head sideways increasing the stretch
     slowly with your other arm. Hold for 10 seconds and
     repeat three times.

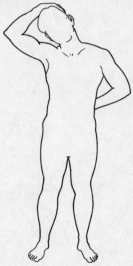

Remember that it takes time to change a disordered
pattern. Initially the important thing is to identify the bad
breathing pattern and understand how to go about
achieving a good pattern.

   How we breathe is truly who we are.

SIX

ARE YOU OVERDRAWN
AT THE BODY BANK?

You have a deep reservoir of natural energy to draw upon, but where is it? And how do you unlock this energy? An increasingly common shorthand scribble on medical records is TATT — tired all the time. If you fall into this category, you can boost your vitality by correcting your breathing.

Think about money for a minute. If you save, you have money to spend. If you spend more than you have saved, you will become overdrawn. And if you continue to overspend, you will become bankrupt. What has this got to do with breathing? Everything.

CASE HISTORY

Mary, aged thirty-seven, is a successful accounts director. She works sixty hours a week, including the odd weekend.

Work is intense with strict deadlines. Mary is exposed to internal pressures — pressure to perform, working as the 'go between', the 'meat in the sandwich' between the 'colourful' creative team and the client, trying to keep both parties happy. She is also exposed to external pressure from clients — trying to meet their high expectations, ensuring that the budget is not exceeded, attending debriefing meetings which must be reported on within twenty-four hours, to name a few.

On top of this Mary has two children, aged seven and nine, and she is heavily involved in the PTA and the children's sports teams. She tries to remain fit with exercise at least four times a week, she eats healthily, and is a supportive friend. She has a housekeeper once a week but often does a quick clean beforehand and is quite particular about the house. She also has a husband who needs some time as well. Wow! Wonder woman — not an uncommon scenario these days.

It is not surprising that Mary gradually began to feel tired and developed muscular aches and pains in her neck and shoulders, the muscle groups most used when working on the computer and when breathing into the upper chest. Her tiredness worsened towards the end of the week but over the weekend Mary found she managed to get a good night's sleep and she recovered. This went on for a period of six months and during this time Mary took on a few more tasks, both at work and outside. She was beginning to appear superhuman, and of course the praise she received kept her going: 'You are so capable', 'You are just amazing with the amount you can do', 'You are my role model — the way you juggle your load is just admirable'. However, Mary was not listening to her body and the warning signs continued.

Mary noticed that she started waking around

three or four in the morning, finding herself wide awake thinking of work. She remembers having the odd headache and starting to become irritable with the children, at times exploding with anger for no reason. Her colleagues realised that she was speeding up. One particular week the workload increased more than usual and Mary found her pain unbearable — she just couldn't think. She walked out of work and was unable to return for a month. Mary was well and truly in overdraft and in fact near bankruptcy.

When I first saw Mary the priority was to show her how to use relaxed breathing. Initially her breathing was chaotic with large volumes into her upper chest, which was heaving as if she had just sprinted a four-minute mile. It is essential to reverse this pattern as soon as possible as it causes the body to tumble further into a state of disarray. If relaxed breathing is not effective initially then a short-term sedative medication may be necessary. After two days of slowing down and having all demands removed Mary began to feel better. Her breathing technique was a major tool to focus on as she became aware that the minute her breathing started to alter from a relaxed pattern it would effectively push her further into exhaustion.

With time and guidance Mary began to improve. As she commented five months later: 'The breathing continues to help me. Whenever I get that "out-of-control" feeling I concentrate on my breathing and go for a walk. It is amazing how what I thought was such a big deal really is not. My world suddenly takes on a calm feeling.'

ARE YOU OVERDRAWN AT THE BODY BANK?

I always emphasise to my patients: '*Never forget where you have just been — never forget how it felt. Do not go there again.* Use the tools you have been equipped with, be gentle with yourself, reserve the energy that is slowly returning for activities that make you feel good.'

People who experience this sort of problem are commonly over-achievers or ambitious perfectionists, so when they begin to feel 'well' again it is very easy for them to start slipping back into old habits. We become so conditioned that it is easy to repeat the same process. Let's face it, we all know how hard it is to save and budget but in the long run it pays off.

My role is somewhat similar to that of a bank manager. Before you even approach your bank manager to ask for that loan extension or to discuss your grim financial state, shaking in your shoes, palms sweaty and mouth dry, you will often know the outcome — a strict budget or a little rearranging but the loan will be fine if you can prove you are able to maintain it.

This scenario is not dissimilar to paying a visit to a health professional. You know you will be asked questions about your health: Have you been eating regularly, sleeping well? Exercising? Relaxing? What are your bowel motions like? Do you feel tired? Do you have a lot of stress in your life? Health professionals are constantly assessing whether patients are in credit or debit — are they well and healthy or rundown and tired — and if so for what reason?

If you happen to be in overdraft, the advice you are given by your health professional will be similar to that given by your bank manager: 'Pull in the reins and try to balance outgoing with incoming.' In other words, a little more rest and sleep to allow recovery to occur.

A powerful tool in my assessment of patients is their breathing pattern.

YOUR BREATHING BANK STATEMENT

Pattern/Credit	Pattern/Debit
Nose	Mouth
Abdomen, lower rib movement	Upper chest, shoulders moving
Regular	Irregular
Rhythmical	Erratic
Soft	Noisy
Rate	Rate
8–12	>18, < 6

Your individual budget will depend on your breathing pattern. For example, a typical patient might present complaining of fatigue, shortness of breath and panic sensations that have continued for a period of at least six months. On assessment the breathing pattern is found to be upper chest, mouth, with a rate of twenty-two per minute. The budget (treatment) would be as follows:

1   Twice daily relaxed breathing practice.

2   Relaxed breathing prior to sleep.

3   Hourly awareness of breathing — ensure you are using effective breathing and that you are able to sustain this for at least three to four breaths. Use the **green dot method** as a reminder.

4   Stretches (see pages 71–75).

5   Relaxed breathing or effective breathing in situations of panic or shortness of breath in order to reverse the sensation; exercises (as described on page 150).

I will often place extremely exhausted patients on a very strict budget, allowing only a specified level of activity and stress to ensure that breathing stays within certain limits. The minute breathing becomes laboured it is important to stop and rest. If someone is totally exhausted he or she must be seen by a medical professional.

If you allow yourself $100 to spend in a week, you will create problems for yourself if you continue to spend once the money is gone. Remember that it takes only one dollar to begin reversing the process. One breath is all it takes. You are the only one who can make the change and become accountable for your own budgeting.

Each day in my clinical practice I see more and more patients who present in overdraft — many are bankrupt. The most common questions asked of me are, 'Why am I so tired? Why do I feel so bad? My doctor says there is nothing wrong. My specialist says I have no disease. I'm beginning to think it's all in my head. What is wrong with me?'

These patients may have seen their GP on several occasions, and specialists may have ruled out any sinister conditions before stress is finally diagnosed. Many people fall in between wellness and ill health — they may be fatigued, exhausted, and lacking vitality. Ideally we should have enough energy to get us through the day and then some in reserve. With a little knowledge, understanding and application it is easy: breathing bridges the gap.

A well-known quote reads: 'Life is not a dress rehearsal.' It saddens me to think that people are not experiencing life to the full. So often patients say to me, 'I just haven't got the energy.' Without natural energy life can be a tough process. However, we all have the capability of increasing the amount we have to spend.

If you experience any of the following you may need to look at the way in which you breathe:

- Shortness of breath

- Fatigue

- Muscle aches and pains

- Sighing and yawning

- Poor concentration

- Headaches

- Insomnia

- Chest pain or tightness

- Feelings of panic or loss of control

- Dizziness

- Pins and needles, numbness

- Gastric reflux, nausea

- Bad breath

- Bloating

- Flatulence

- Anxiety
- 'Electric shock' feeling
- Eye strain
- Vivid dreams, nightmares
- Foggy head
- Temperature changes
- Irritable cough
- Racing heart

These are the most common signs and symptoms associated with a bad breathing pattern.

There is a strong relationship between breathing and energy. We have been introduced to this in Chapter Four. To explain this further I will introduce you to the 'human performance curve' on page 87. This represents our body bank and demonstrates the energy–breathing link. A disordered breathing pattern can shift you towards the right-hand side of the curve which can predispose you to ill health. When using this graph we talk about stimulus versus performance. 'Stimulus' can mean demand, stress or arousal. In this case it means any demand that is placed upon us, whether physical or mental.

Stress is a much-used word in today's society. It is not uncommon to hear comments such as, 'I am so stressed' or 'Don't worry about Bob, he's just stressed'. Stress can be good or bad. It is a necessity of life and without it we would end up permanent couch potatoes spending our lives at level 1 on the human performance curve, achieving nothing.

When looking at the human performance curve, 'good' stress is represented on the left-hand side of the curve and 'bad' stress on the right-hand side. As stress increases, so does our performance, but only to a point (our threshold). Beyond this point, any further increase in demand causes performance to decrease.

The body recognises and stores stress long before the conscious mind registers it. Do not underestimate the amount of energy that is used up holding on to physical and emotional stress. Emotional stress is perceived by the body as a physical threat. The minute we are challenged, our diaphragm contracts, our breathing alters and the body readies itself for the perceived oncoming threat. If the threat continues, the rest of the body tenses, the nervous system is stimulated and adrenaline begins to pour into the body. It is ready for action. Often people are quite oblivious to this and will only register when stronger signs and symptoms appear, for example, the heart pumps rapidly, the palms become sweaty, and the chest tightens. Awareness is very important (see Chapter Seven).

It is not until the body and finally the diaphragm relax that all the effects of emotional strain are dissipated. That is why when people begin to change their breathing from a bad pattern to a relaxed one it is not uncommon to experience some emotion — anything from crying to uncontrollable laughter.

Your placement on the human performance curve is a good guide to your breathing pattern. If you are on the left-hand side of the curve, you are breathing effectively. If you are on the right-hand side you are probably breathing badly.

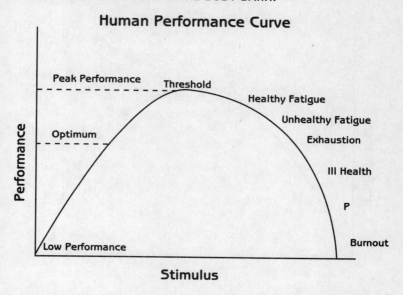

The human performance curve (used with permission of Dr Peter Nixon, cardiologist, London).

If increased demands (physical or mental) are placed on the body the breathing pattern alters. If these demands are met by a supply of energy the breathing pattern will remain rhythmical. When you reach the point where there is less energy than the demand requires you will go over the top of the curve into healthy fatigue. At this point the breathing pattern becomes rigid, larger in volume, and faster, worsening and often becoming irregular and erratic as you progress further down the right-hand side of the curve. We all go over the top of the curve into healthy fatigue at times, for example, upon completing that big project, finishing a triathlon or writing a book, and this is normal and healthy. However, once you have gone over into fatigue you must

Human Performance Curve

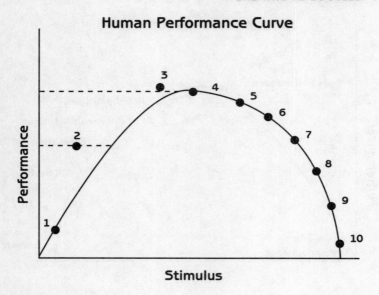

stop and allow recovery to occur. If you continue to push, you will go into 'bad' fatigue and this in turn leads to exhaustion, ill health, and eventually burnout.

The human performance curve can be used to symbolise a day, a year, several years, or a simple task, for example, running. Initially it may be a little difficult (1), then you become used to it (2), you crank up the pace, adrenaline starts to rush (3), you reach peak performance and are feeling great (4), you continue and gradually begin to tire (good fatigue) (5), you continue and begin to stumble a little (bad fatigue) (6), you persist and are now spending too much and falling into overdraft. This is a common sight at the end of a marathon — people struggling to the finish line, vomiting with exhaustion (7). It usually takes time to reach 8 and 9 on the curve but if you continue to push you will eventually end up with ill health (8), for example, a stomach ulcer, irritable bowel disease or a painful syndrome such as occupational over-use syndrome. If you don't stop at this point (9) you collapse and burn out, becoming bankrupt (10).

HUMAN PERFORMANCE CURVE

Stimulus: Any demand (stress) placed on us (mental or physical)

Performance: Output (mental or physical)

1 **Low performance**/low stimulation.

2 **Optimum: Healthy tension**/optimum level of performance.

3 **Peak performance**.

4 **Threshold**: The point at which we have reached our full potential. Beyond this point increased stimulus or demand will lower our performance. At this stage, recovery will return us to the left-hand side of the curve. Recovery comes in many forms including effective relaxed breathing.

5 **Healthy fatigue:** Physical or mental tiredness; inability to give a normal response until recovery has occurred. It can relate to the whole person, to one organ or to tissue such as muscle. It commonly occurs when we have achieved something to the best of our ability. In this state we feel tired and know we need sleep and rest to recover. At this point also natural energy starts to diminish and we begin to rely on adrenaline to keep us going. Breathing will

become disordered and remain that way as long as you are on the right-hand side of the curve.

6 **Unhealthy fatigue:** At this stage we often ignore the warning signs and continue to push. We become increasingly tired and begin to experience muscular aches and pains, sleep becomes disturbed, we become irritable and start experiencing mood swings. These signs are a built-in mechanism that serve as a warning to stop, just as when we are hungry our stomach rumbles, or when we are cold our hairs stand on end. When we have gone over our threshold into fatigue we must stop and allow recovery. Unfortunately, many people in western cultures ignore such warning signs — we have been programmed to continue, conditioned to believe that it is a weakness to stop and rest. As a consequence we often don't listen to our bodies until it is too late. It is common here to see an increase in the use of stimulants such as alcohol, coffee and cigarettes.

Fatigue presents in many forms. In the workplace over the last decade conditions such as occupational over-use syndrome have swept through New Zealand and Australia. Chronic fatigue and chronic pain syndromes, Gulf War syndrome and hyperventilation syndrome have also become increasingly common. Fatigue is believed to be the epidemic of the twenty-first century.

7 **Exhaustion:** At this stage there are no reserves of energy for coping with the unexpected. It is difficult to cope with change or any further demands. Self-esteem falls, tension rises, aggression flares, motiva-

tion wanes, you become more accident-prone. Poor coping tactics are often implemented. Sleep deprivation is accepted as 'normal'. Breathing is quite chaotic and will become more disordered as the individual pushes harder. It is almost at a point where it is beyond easy recovery.

8 **Ill health:** Conditions such as irritable bowel syndrome, gastric reflux, hiatus hernia, migraines, anxiety states, phobic or heart disorders may begin to plague you. Rapid beating sensations of the heart, raised blood pressure, fluid retention and a disturbed immune system are all common. Symptoms will depend on the individual's circumstances and are often age dependent. Some people remain in this state for many years.

9 **P:** The point at which normal rest will not allow recovery to occur. Patients in this category are often medicated or removed from all demands. When I worked with merchant bankers in London, if they reached this point they would be sent to the Greek islands for a recovery period of at least three weeks — no work, family, phone, email, fax or traffic; only sun, sleep and food. It would be nice if we could all do this. However, the main aim is to remove all stimuli and demands, as this is the point at which even the smallest of things could cause a tip into burnout.

10 **Burnout:** Breakdown, inability to cope or function. When working with survivors of torture nearly all had 'burnout'. The torture process broke people down both mentally and physically. Victims had often been

subjected to days of sleep deprivation, little food, extremes of temperature, interrogation and threats, all within a short period of time. The body shuts down and switches off in order to protect itself. It is a long road back to recovery. Breathing is chaotic. Changes in breathing when the body has been pushed to extremes can in fact enable the person to survive. At this stage it is necessary to remove all stimuli and use medication to help rebalance the body. Breathing instruction can then be given to assist with the return to healthy functioning and wellness.

CASE HISTORY

Martin, aged thirty-five, is a partner in a financial planning company and has two young children. Over a period of two years he found himself under increasing pressure. His workload and hours of work increased, his dietary habits changed and exercise decreased. Martin ended up suffering from burnout. One day in the office the phone went and he walked away from it and did not return for six months. Martin commented: 'I thought I was bullet-proof but I think the body said, "If you are not going to give me a rest I'll fix you!"' On reflection Martin said that he had been aware of warning signs over the last two years, but he had put them down to viruses.

Martin has a strong sporting background in squash, rowing, triathlons and weight training, and always relied on his body to cope when he physically pushed himself to the limit. He really did believe he was invincible. But increasing demands over a long period eventually brought him to his knees.

One of the first things that changes in response to increased demand is the way we breathe. All patients on the right side of the curve present with a bad breathing pattern. This is frequently seen in times of war — it is well documented that war induces stress and has a devastating effect on a person both physically and psychologically.

In World War I and World War II the impact of fatigue upon industry and the economy was so great that research committees were established to study the problem. They reported that 'an enduring degradation of health and performance results when fatigue is carried slightly beyond the point where rest can provide sound physiological recuperation', in other words, exhaustion and burnout. At this point, normal rest (sleep, breathing, relaxation) will not allow recovery. Soldiers had to be removed from all stimuli, sometimes requiring sedation in order to recover. Some fortunates were sent to recuperate in health spas for a period of about six weeks.

Such studies have identified two types of people: those who push themselves day after day and who eventually collapse in sheer exhaustion, and those who collapse before even making it to the front line of action. Both groups of people experienced the same clinical signs and symptoms, both having gone 'over the top'. This highlights the difference in a person's threshold, according to Dr Ian Pogson of Primary Corporate Health. A number of factors play a role in determining a person's resilience or ability to cope with physical and psychological demands:

1   Personal health: Breathing, sleep, diet, exercise.

2   Personal awareness of warning signs and symptoms.

3   Relationships: At work, home, with friends and support people.

4   Environment: Time management processes.

5   Thought processes: Learned thoughts, self-esteem, perception of events, patterns of behaviour.

It is predicted the twenty-first century will be a time of increased demands, and survival will depend on resilience. It is thought that by the year 2020 depression and heart disease will be the leading ailments and it is well known that both of these can be attributed to stress. Stress is alive and well and a fact of life — it is not going to go away, so we must learn to live with it and adapt accordingly. The only certainty in the twenty-first century is that of change — we can either see this as a threat or we can meet the challenge. The good news is that we all have the ability to learn coping skills.

SEVEN

WHAT ARE YOUR
WARNING SIGNS?

QUIZ TIME

Q When you get tense, what part of your body stores the tension?

A _____

Q What part tenses first?

A _____

Q What happens to your breathing in these situations?

A _____

Q What are your warning signs and symptoms when you become fatigued?

A _____

Q What situations cause you to become tense?

A _____

Answering these questions will help you learn to listen to your body and take appropriate action.

WHAT ARE YOUR WARNING SIGNS?

My patients complain of a host of signs and symptoms:

- Fatigue, exhaustion

- Muscular aches and pains, pins and needles, 'electric shock' feeling

- Shortness of breath, inability to get a 'good' breath, inability to hold one's breath

- Raised temperature

- Headache, dizziness or detached sensations, loss of memory, foggy head

- Chest pain, palpitations, chest tightness

- Photophobia, visual disturbance

- Digestive problems, reflux, belching, flatulence, constricting sensations in the throat

- Increased frequency of urination, waking during the night needing to urinate

- Anxiety

- Insomnia, waking after about four hours with anxiety and panic and sometimes chest pain or cardiac arrhythmia

- Cold hands, cold feet

It is very important to recognise your warning signs and symptoms. Awareness is one of the first steps to prevention. **The following questionnaire is a guide to your fatigue status.** The scale will reflect your level of fatigue:

Score: Frequently = 3 ; Often = 2; Seldom = 1; Never = 0

	Frequently	Often	Seldom	Never
1 Do you feel sleepy whilst at work?				
2 Do you have problems getting to sleep?				
3 Do you wake in the morning feeling unrefreshed?				
4 Do you often feel tired during the day?				
5 Do you find it difficult to concentrate on problems?				
6 Do you have frequent headaches?				
7 Do you have frequent colds, earaches or sore throats?				
8 Do you have persistent pains in your joints?				
9 Do you experience digestive problems, eg, nausea, reflux, irregular bowel motions?				
10 Are you often irritable?				
11 Do you have nervous feelings or feelings of anxiety?				
12 Do you feel lethargic?				
Total				

0–10 = Healthy.

11–18 = Healthy Fatigue: Stop, rest and recover.

19–30 = Unhealthy Fatigue: Action is needed —
recovery will take more than a couple of
days to work towards a balanced lifestyle.
See 'Longer Relaxed Breathing', pages 55–58.

31–36 = Exhaustion: Seek medical assistance
immediately.

Scale of Signs and Symptoms of Living on the Right-Hand Side of the Human Performance Curve

Breathing pattern disorders are associated with each stage.

FATIGUE

Tiredness

Aching muscles

Poor balance

Poor memory

Breathing: Slightly altered.

UNHEALTHY FATIGUE

Fidgeting, clock watching, crossing arms, clenching fists, tensing shoulders, clenching jaw

Poor sleep

Very tired

Aches and pains

Headache

Backache

Diarrhoea

Constipation

Mood changes

Shortness of breath
Flare in allergies
Sore throat
Nasal congestion
Breathing: Faster, less pause between breaths,
inspiration time = expiration time, breathing into
upper chest.

EXHAUSTION
Insomnia
Increased anxiety
Increased blood pressure
Detached feeling
Palpitations
Memory loss
Rapid mood swings
Dizziness
Loss of balance
Spaced feeling
Laryngitis
Chest pain
Breathing: Difficult, no pause, inspiration often >
expiration, heavy sighs, definite breaks in rhythm,
definite awareness of a problem.

ILL HEALTH
Irritable bowel
Ulcer
Heart disease
Problems with blood pressure
Depression
Anxiety

Bronchitis
Sinusitis
Breathing: Dependent on the disorder.

BURNOUT
Inability to cope
No energy
Unable to think
Unable to get out of bed
Total shutdown
Not enough air
Breathing: Large volumes, chaotic, erratic pattern, totally disordered.

THE HUMAN PERFORMANCE CURVE CHECKLIST
Refer to curve on pages 87, 88.

ARE YOU ON THE DOWN SLOPE?

Because too much is demanded of you?

Because you cannot say 'no' when you should?

Because you are not sufficiently in control? Can't cope?

— Too angry, too tense, too upset, too irritable, too indignant?

— Too much people-poisoning?

— Too many time pressures? Too impatient?

Because you are not sleeping well enough to keep well?

Because you are not keeping fit enough to stay well?

Because you are not balancing the periods of hard effort with adequate sleep and relaxation?

Because you are out of real energy and using sheer will-power to keep going?

Because you are infallible, indispensable, indestructible, immortal?

To return to the banking analogy, when you breathe with a regulated breathing pattern you are making money. The slower and more relaxed the rate and rhythm, the more you make. However, we must spend money to live, just as we must stimulate our breathing pattern. As both physical and mental demands are placed upon us our breathing patterns change. Increased demands result in larger breaths, upper chest breathing and often mouth breathing. The air flow and rate of breathing increase.

Imagine yourself running up a flight of stairs. As you climb without rest you become increasingly short of breath. As the demand increases your breathing becomes laboured until eventually you reach your destination and can recover. Your level of fitness will determine the speed at which you recover. Some people will fatigue before reaching the top and will either slow down or pause in order to complete the remaining stairs without collapsing. Others will refuse to stop, risking bankruptcy. Remember, energy is finite. It is a case of supply and demand. If supply is greater than demand, recovery is not required but if the supply becomes less than the demand, recovery is essential.

The following is a guideline to expected recovery times based on my clinical experience:

FATIGUE: A couple of days.
UNHEALTHY FATIGUE: One week.
EXHAUSTION: Six to eight weeks.
ILL HEALTH: Dependent on the condition.
BURNOUT: Eight months to three years.

Why is recovery so important? As illustrated by the human performance curve, if we do not go 'over the top' sometimes we are probably not stretching ourselves enough. But we will only achieve the endurance to keep going and going if we allow adequate time for the body to repair and regenerate. This applies to all ages. I have treated an eight-year-old and a ninety-six-year-old patient with the same techniques and both recovered well.

EIGHT

BREATHING TO INCREASE
YOUR PERFORMANCE
AND RECOVERY

One of New Zealand rugby's most consistent goal kickers was Grant Fox. But it was not always so. According to Fox: *'After an Auckland versus Sydney game in 1984, I was bitterly disappointed with my kicking. Jim Blair, our fitness trainer, told me that I was trying too hard. I needed to relax my body and focus the mind.'* Fox recounts the simple breathing routine that Blair gave him: *'Breathe in for one, breathe out for one. Breathe in for two, breathe out for two. Breathe in for three and out for three. Then head down and go. Since retiring from the game I still use the routine when I need to relax. I find it particularly useful when I have difficulty in getting to sleep.'*

Breathing has long been recognised as a crucial component of athletic performance. For example, when athletes wish to increase speed they will alter their breathing to large, explosive breaths that are syncronised with their stride. The breath increases in proportion to the energy output. When athletes wish to sustain endurance such as in marathon running they will maintain a consistent rhythm of breathing throughout

BREATHING TO INCREASE YOUR PERFORMANCE

the event. This allows a continuous release of energy. To increase performance the breath must be rhythmical, even in volume and tailored to the task required.

Long-distance runners who have problems with partially blocked noses are especially prone to breathing disorders. Good diagnosis is required, and correction may involve surgery, breathing retraining or nasal hygiene.

SPRINTING: JAN'S STORY

'I have been a competitive person since childhood and have been a New Zealand secondary schools representative in the 200m sprint and in women's netball. From the age of eleven or twelve I trained five nights a week. I was well conditioned to the pattern of breathing that is used in sprinting — it became my "norm". The pattern was that of an over-expanded upper chest, breathing in large volumes of air, and actively forcing the breath out. The adrenaline created was helpful for top-level competition as it gave you the edge.

'But no one stated the obvious — that I should not breathe like that normally. The "on switch" was triggered and I didn't know where the "off switch" was, or even that there was one. Now I understand why my joints ached in class, and I would often find myself hitting them to distract from the pain. I frequently had sharp pains in my chest and between my ribs and I thought they were normal! They would disappear when training or competing — so I figured I just needed to do more. I did not realise that I was reinforcing the bad cycle.

*'My sleep was often disturbed and it could take
me one or two hours to get to sleep, as by bedtime I
was wide awake. When my body tried to tell me how
tired it really was, I just thought I needed to get going
again.*

*'My body eventually started to break down —
injuries did not heal so quickly and in the end I just
couldn't force myself to compete any longer.*

*'I ceased competitive sport and redirected the
challenge to physiotherapy training. By then my
breathing pattern was completely reversed, making
me more vulnerable to minor demands.'*

At rest Jan's breathing pattern did not meet the activity.
As a consequence, too much adrenaline flowed into her
body, causing symptoms while at rest. When she ran,
the breathing matched the activity. It is not uncommon
for top athletes to have bad breathing patterns when
they retire.

RUGBY

The advent of professional rugby in New Zealand has
led to increased pressures on team members. According
to David Abercrombie, physiotherapist to the All Blacks:
*'With the increased frequency of training and games we
have seen a steady increase in speed, strength and
aerobic fitness as well as an increase in the frequency
of injuries. The pressures on position and the need for
maintaining high levels of intense competition week
after week have had a noticeable effect on both the
physical and psychological aspects of players. As we are
aware, all sports people suffer from bad periods. It is*

BREATHING TO INCREASE YOUR PERFORMANCE

always hard to blame an increase in injuries on any one factor, but with rugby at present we have a number of factors that could all contribute to the current situation.'

The increased demand for both mental and physical agility make it extremely important to maintain a healthy human performance curve — constant measuring of supply and demand and ensuring that recovery is optimal.

Breathing well will assist in quick recovery. It can help with relaxation and focusing, both on and off the field. It can also be used to maximise energy expenditure, as players require endurance. When a player runs around for eighty minutes, constantly mouth breathing and with shoulders hunched up around the neck, energy is used quickly. However, if mouth breathing is regularly interspersed with nose breathing and body tension kept to a minimum, energy can be reserved.

GOLF

Golfer Peter Fowler, past Australian, New Zealand and World Cup Open winner, comments: *'When you hit the ball use your breathing to help with concentration, for example, breathe in, swing up, breathe out, one, two, three, as you swing out. This assists with rhythm and accurate biomechanics. It is also very useful in between holes to help calm the performance nerves. Breathing enables you to focus and concentrate on what you are doing. Trainers often talk about breathing freely — this increases your performance.'*

TENNIS

A tennis professional stated: *'When I walk back behind the court I focus on my breathing. This allows time for energy repletion and relaxation.'* The controversial 'grunt' that Monica Seles lets out as she hits the ball may be noisy but the explosive breath out increases the energy released and increases the force at which she can deliver the ball to her opponent.

HORSE RIDING

Catherine, aged thirty-four, is a competitive equestrian rider. She comments: *'The most interesting thing I've learnt is that when I breathe well my horse is so easy to control. When he is misbehaving and not responding I realise that I've either been holding my breath or breathing so shallowly and rigidly that he has obviously responded to my tension.'*

DIVING

Breathing is used to fine tune buoyancy. A device called a BCD (buoyancy control device) enables the diver to drop to the depths desired or to rise up. The BCD can be inflated using air from the tank or air can be released as necessary. Once stabilised at the level you want to cruise at, you can then use your breath to fine tune your movement and save air from your tanks. For example, if you are cruising along and come across some rocks, breathing in more air will allow you to rise up and travel over them. A shallower breath or breathing out all the air will lower you.

Breathing technique is also useful to relax you. Many novice divers 'chew' through their air as they are nervous and unfamiliar with the process and tend to breathe rapidly. A regulated and relaxed breathing pattern will use far less air.

People who have an upper chest, large volume breathing pattern often comment that they find it difficult to stay on the bottom of a pool but that they have no problems floating.

BOXING

Breathe out when you throw the punch to release maximum energy.

MARTIAL ARTS

This excellent discipline combines the breath well with physical and mental exercises. Practitioners of Chinese martial arts say that if the untrained body were as erratic in its movements as the untrained mind, a man would be lucky to come through a day unscathed. They believe that a trained body is impossible without a trained mind and use the process of meditation to attain this.

YOGA

This is another discipline that combines breathing and movement. Both these disciplines presume an individual has a 'good' breathing pattern. Often if you have a bad pattern it is advisable to correct this prior to commencing these practices.

SWIMMING

Breathing control is very important when swimming. The breathing must be co-ordinated with the body movement. Swimming is an excellent exercise for developing the lungs and co-ordinating breathing — I often suggest it to my patients.

WEIGHT-LIFTING
It is recommended that you breathe in as you lift the weight, as this increases the support to the trunk region, thus protecting the back.

PERFORMANCE ANXIETY
This can affect anyone, whether competing at the Olympics, going for a job interview or standing in front of the class to read out homework. Prior to the event the throat constricts, the stomach begins to tighten, the hands become clammy, the voice begins to quiver, and breathing speeds up. At worst, panic may set in — breathing becomes more laboured, thoughts become disturbed, and palpitations, dizziness, nausea and even vomiting may occur. You are petrified of losing control. Increased anxiety acts as a feedback loop.

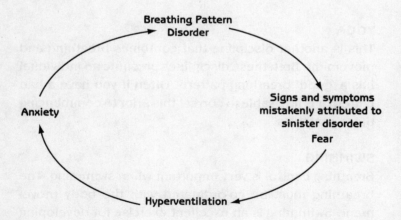

BREATHING TO INCREASE YOUR PERFORMANCE

One might well ask why we do it.

Almost every performer is familiar with the symptoms. In the theatre it is known as 'stage fright' and many actors use breathing techniques as a means of control; in business it is often perceived as a weakness. However, it is well known that moderate levels of anxiety can enhance performance. The important factor is your ability to regulate these feelings so that you are in control. Breathing is one of your most powerful tools. Break the cycle!

Try using the following exercise before a performance:

1 In standing or sitting position focus on your feet.

2 Think about your toes, your heels and your inner arch. Feel these areas on the ground beneath you.

3 Ease the tension in your knees, even jiggle them a few times.

4 Allow your shoulders and jaw to drop.

5 Now think about your breathing.

6 Focus on breathing in through your nose and feeling your stomach rise.

7 Let the air out.

9 Pause.

10 Continue until you feel in control and focused.

11 You are now ready to perform.

Singers and wind-instrument players can be predisposed to breathing disorders. The nature of their profession leads them to learn to control their breathing well — in some cases almost too well, leading to constant over-breathing. The most important thing for these groups is to learn to use relaxed breathing when not performing.

BREATHING FOR RECOVERY
Relaxation is the flip side of performance. Research shows that breathing strategies are critical in the effectiveness of all relaxation techniques.

PAIN CONTROL
Connective tissue pervades every structure of the body. It contracts in response to any stressful stimuli — sudden trauma, chronic emotional stress, pathology, deprivation, etc. Over time this can result in pain and affect the efficient functioning of the structure. It is well documented in medical literature that relaxation and breathing strategies reduce pain significantly. The instant you feel pain increasing, stop and do eight relaxed breaths. If you have a chronic pain problem you should do the longer relaxed breathing on page 55 twice a day.

POST SPORT
Good breathing increases the oxygen flow to muscles, helping to remove the waste products generated by intense activity. It is vital, post sport, to slow down the task breathing ratio to allow the body time to readjust back to normal. If you do not you run the risk of a mismatch, often causing an episode of hyperventilation

and with it a host of unpleasant signs and symptoms.

When stretching to 'cool down' or 'warm up' always remember to breathe out when you stretch out. Hold the stretch for a few seconds at the end of the range, breathe out and stretch a little further.

SLEEP

Breathing and sleep are mentioned throughout the book. It is vital in order for quality sleep to occur that our breathing is nose, low, slow and rhythmical. Recent literature has stated that if we think about our breathing prior to sleep and even if we do not breathe correctly it will release a hormone called melatonin. This hormone is responsible for regulating the body's sleep/wake cycle.

RECOVERY ON THE
HUMAN PERFORMANCE CURVE

B – Breathe well

A – Arousal decreased

L – Lots of water

A – A 'good' night's sleep

N – Nutrition balanced

C – Calm mind

E – Exercise and movement

NINE

BREATHING AND
THE WORKPLACE

The industrial era brought inventions that freed up our time — automatic washing machines, dryers and cell phones to name a few. However, we are still squeezing more into a day than ever before, many of us working much longer and harder. Work analysts predict that unsettling changes within the workforce will continue for the next five to ten years.

Work has become the focus in many people's lives as we strive to keep up in a materialistic society driven by market forces. As a result it is common practice to see both partners working, where in the past one stayed at home carrying out the duties involved in running a home and family. This role now has to be juggled by both partners, which adds further pressures.

Corporate executives are being exposed to increasing stress and frequently show symptoms of overload. What starts at the top of a company often trickles down the line.

As we move into the era of computerisation and cyberspace there are problems on the horizon. We are becoming more sedentary — thinking more, perhaps,

BREATHING AND THE WORKPLACE

but using our bodies less. We may communicate all day with a computer screen, becoming so absorbed as the day goes on that our shoulders tense, our breathing changes, we end up thinking faster and faster until our brain resembles a spinning top, and then exhaustion sets in — but it is now time to go home — to our partner, children or friends, to cook dinner, walk the dog, do those home handyman jobs!

Some survival tools are necessary.

BUSINESS MEETINGS

Business meetings are so often held in hot, stuffy rooms where coffee is served and there is a lot of talking. These factors rapidly drop carbon dioxide levels, switching on the sympathetic nervous system and potentially causing some uncomfortable symptoms — the last thing you want during an important meeting. The following will be helpful:

1 Prior to the meeting: Stop; breathe through the nose with low, slow breaths for inner calm.

2 Walk into the meeting at a regular, rhythmical pace — don't rush.

3 Sit well back in your chair, making sure that you are sitting on your bottom bones and not your tailbone. Keep your lower back supported and your shoulders back and down. (This is excellent positioning for good breathing — it also looks strong.)

4 When speaking use pauses — respect the commas and fullstops, breathing out as you do so.

5   Drink water rather than coffee.

PRESENTATION SKILLS

Remaining relaxed keeps you in control at all times. A relaxed, confident presenter will relax those who are listening. Prior to speaking, ground yourself:

1   In sitting or standing position, focus on your feet. Plant them firmly on the ground. Notice that your shoulders drop instantly — if you are focusing on your feet you cannot tense your shoulders.

2   Breathe out. Envisage breathing out through your feet.

3   Breathing in through your nose, expand your lower rib cage and then your upper chest. Hold for a second.

4   Exhale all the air.

5   Pause.

6   Repeat the exercise once more.

Throughout your presentation bring yourself back to your feet. Ensure that when you talk you respect punctuation.

JOB INTERVIEWS

The following exercise will help reduce anxiety prior to a job interview:

1   In standing or sitting position focus on your feet.

2   Think about your toes, your heels and your inner

arch, feeling them on the ground beneath you.

3 Relax your knees, jiggling them a few times.

4 Allow your shoulders and jaw to drop.

5 Now think about your breathing. Focus on breathing in through your nose, allowing your stomach to rise.

6 Release the air.

7 Pause.

8 Continue until you feel in control and focused.

You are now ready.

CONFLICT

When you find yourself in any situation of conflict, for example, on the telephone to that difficult customer or a tense situation with your boss:

1 Stop.

2 Breathe out.

3 Inhale through the nose — think 'low and slow'.

4 Pause to regain your composure and clear your head. Do not let the other person get the better of you — ultimately the winner is the person who 'keeps cool'.

5 Continue to use low, slow breathing until you feel calmer.

SHARPENING PERCEPTION

It is easy to allow your thoughts to drift or to fill your mind with many concepts — these both decrease your ability to focus. Western man has developed the bad habit of thinking too much and ignoring his body, and this can lead to overloading of the brain. Thoughts can sometimes speed up to a point where all clarity is lost. It is important to rest your mind from time to time to enable you to re-focus.

A few years ago I was working with Japanese bankers on a stress management programme. It was not un-common for them to stop and appear to go into a trance for a few seconds — what they were doing was breathing into their 'hara' or abdomen. They believed this gave them the ability to focus and increase their perception.

UPON COMPLETING A TASK OR PROJECT

Stop; sigh out. Literally 'taking a breath' before begin-ning the next project is worth its weight in gold. Do it often — research suggests every fifty minutes. Stop, breathe out, pause to still your mind and body for a second, then continue as before. If in doubt, breathe out — it will create movement, release tension, rest your brain and re-energise with fresh, oxygenated blood.

SWITCHING OFF

If you have a problem 'switching off' your brain, relaxed breathing is an excellent way to achieve this, especially prior to sleep. The aim is to get out of your thoughts and into your body. See the technique for relaxed breathing on page 52.

BREATHING AND THE WORKPLACE

RECOMMENDED HOURLY ROUTINE FOR *ALL* SEDENTARY WORKERS

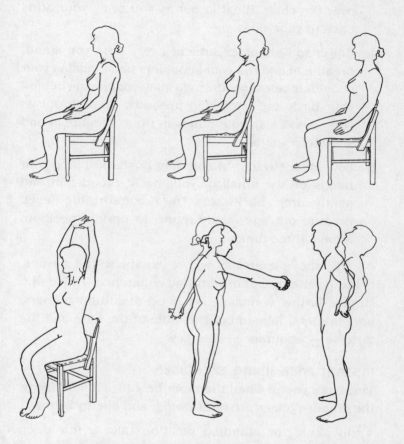

1   Chin tucks: In standing or sitting position, glide your head backwards, pulling your chin towards your neck. Repeat three times.

2   Roll your shoulders backwards in a complete circle three times.

3 Chest stretch: Breathe in, clasping your hands over your head and arching your upper back and arms over the chair. Breathe out as you bring your arms back to your sides.

4 Chest and shoulder stretch: Every time you stand, breathe in and roll your shoulders back, pulling your shoulderblades together, clasping your hands behind your back and stretching upwards. Breathe out as you relax. Clasp your hands in front, breathe in and stretch forwards.

5 Low back stretch: In standing position, place your hands on the small of your back. Breathe in and gently arch backwards to a comfortable level. Breathe out and gently return to upright position. Repeat three times.

The above exercises will re-oxygenate the tissues, restoring energy and maximising endurance. Those who survive in the workplace are good marathon runners, not sprinters. Remember the fable of the hare and the tortoise — endurance is the key.

INSTANT ENERGISING EXERCISES

These are useful when the brain becomes a little foggy, the creative juices are not flowing, and energy is low.

1 In sitting or standing position take a few deep abdominal breaths: Breathing in through your nose, expand your lower rib cage and then the upper chest. Hold for a second.

2 Exhale all the air.

3 Repeat.

BREATHING AND THE WORKPLACE

1   In sitting position, breathe in and out three times at the speed of in one and out two, drawing the abdomen out as you breath in and drawing the abdomen in as you breathe out. Use a forced breath.

These exercises remove stale air and bring fresh oxygen to the body, waking up tired cells.

INSTANT ENERGISING STRETCHES

1   Stand with your feet shoulder-width apart.

2   Tail tuck (tilt your pelvis backwards, literally tucking your tail between your legs).

3   Inhale and lift both arms above your head, interlocking your fingers and stretching upwards.

4   As you breathe out let your arms return to your sides.

5   Repeat three times (see page 64).

1   Stand with your feet shoulder-width apart.

2   Tail tuck.

3   Inhale and stretch your arms and shoulderblades forward at shoulder height.

4   Exhale and stretch your arms, pulling your shoulder-blades together behind your back.

5   Repeat three times (see page 65).

EXERCISES FOR ALL COMPUTER USERS

First, try the following: In sitting position, pretend you are working at a computer. Start using the keyboard and think about the work you are doing. Think about how engrossed you are becoming — keep typing, typing, typing . . . go, go, go . . . now stop. What happened to your breathing? Did you hold your breath?

As a general rule the strongest and fittest amongst us are those who work outdoors in physical jobs. Computerisation and other labour-saving machines mean that many of us move much less than previously. Children spend more play time on computer games. Not only is this action restrictive but the games often require intense concentration, causing adrenaline to pump, muscles to tense and the breath to be held.

The human body is designed to be active. Research has now demonstrated that it is harmful to spend a lot of time sitting, and it is even worse to be braced at a computer. There has been a significant rise in computer-related musculoskeletal pain and injuries. These are often labelled as 'occupational overuse', 'repetitive strain disorders' or 'cumulative trauma disorders'.

An average keyboarding speed is sixty words a minute. Certain groups are required to perform higher speeds, for example, legal secretaries average seventy words a minute, personal assistants eighty words a minute, data entry personnel and banking processors 100–120 words a minute. Faster speeds can be likened to sprinting and time must be allowed for recovery. 'Micropauses' are essential.

Ergonomics (design of the work station) has received a lot of publicity. But there is no point in having an ergonomically efficient set-up if the individual using it is unaware of his or her body tension, movement and breathing pattern. It is important to consider your relationship with your worksite.

As discussed earlier, breath holding and muscle tension consume large amounts of energy. It does not take long to go over the threshold into muscle fatigue. Muscle soreness is an indictor of fatigue — it is not normal. If you plan to continue with an activity throughout the day it is important to assess how you are doing it.

Extensive research carried out in the United States has linked disordered breathing patterns to problems such as occupational overuse as a result of extensive use of computers. Erik Peper and others in an article, 'Repetitive Strain Injury: Electromyography Applications in Physical Therapy' conclude: 'At present workstation ergonomic analysis, proper positioning of furniture and equipment, different mice and keyboards, periodic rest may help reduce physical harm.' However, this approach lacks two crucial elements:

● Kinesthetic awareness (body movement awareness).

● Development of skills to inhibit inappropriate and excessive bracing during task performance. Breathing is an essential tool in this awareness.

Peper continues: 'The computer user must learn to reduce tension and relax muscles when they are not used for the task; the user must also learn skills to sense muscle tension.' He lists the risk patterns to be:

● Asymmetry in body activity, for example, increased use of the mouse in one hand.

● Increased use of muscle tension during a rotational movement, for example, use of upper shoulder muscles in typing and turning at the same time.

● Breath holding or very shallow breathing during movements.

● Lack of awareness of breath holding.

● Lack of awareness of body bracing and asymmetrical muscle use patterns.

So what can we do to increase our awareness of muscle tension and breathing patterns?

1   *Reduce work arousal* (physical and mental demands) by establishing a good breathing pattern (see relaxed and effective breathing, Chapter Five) and implementing it during tasks and breaks.

2   *Take momentary regenerative breaks.* The micro breaks are much more important than the muscle tension during the task. Sustained muscle activity of greater than thirty seconds needs a regenerative break of one to two seconds of low activity. If recovery is not allowed this has an accumulative effect. It has been said that if you work at a keyboard constantly for fifty minutes without a break it will take eight hours for the muscles to recover.

3   *Develop muscle strength,* flexibility and symmetry appropriate for the task.

EXERCISES FOR HIGH USE OF THE COMPUTER

The most important thing is to train yourself to stop regularly. Most people become so engrossed in what they are doing that they lose awareness of time and, worst of all, their body.

When we breathe we are moving; if we are breath holding we are not. This static tension stops fresh blood from flowing to the tissues and prevents removal of waste products. Tissues become brittle, painful and unhealthy.

THE FAMOUS MICROPAUSE
Every three minutes:

1 Stop, breathe out and drop your shoulders.

2 Breathe in through your nose.

3 Breathe out through your nose, dropping your shoulders, jaw and tongue and shaking your hands. Purse your lips as if to whistle in order to exhale the last bit of air.

4 Pause, then continue.

Aim to achieve body and mind relaxation — 'instant calmness'. **The most important thing to do during a micropause is *breathe.***

When you return to the keyboard take note of your breathing and your body tension. Be aware of the intensity at which you hit the keyboard and the tension you use when gripping the mouse. If you are feeling tense, do some relaxed breathing before continuing. *Never* use the excuse that you are too busy to stop. Too busy for what? Your health?

THE LONGER MICROPAUSE

I recommend doing this every half hour. Remember to breathe out when you stretch out. Hold each stretch for 10 seconds.

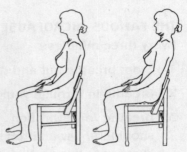

1 Chin tucks: In sitting position glide your head backwards, pulling your chin towards your neck. Glide back, hold and let go. Repeat three times.

2 Side bends: Place your right ear on your right shoulder, breathe out and stretch, then your left ear on your left shoulder. Repeat twice on each side.

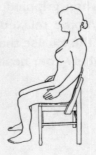

3 Roll your shoulders in a complete circle backwards three times.

4 Place one arm horizontal, and with elbow bent stretching across your body. An excellent stretch for the shoulder-blade muscles.

5 Place your hands behind your back and stretch backwards opening out your chest.

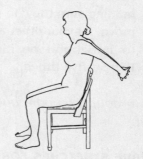

6 Forearm stretches: (a) with your arms turned inwards, pull your hands backwards; (b) turn arm over and stretch palm of hand towards your fore-arm.

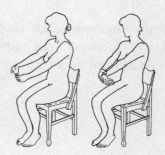

7 Stretch and shake your fingers.

8 Strengthening for the lower shoulderblade muscles: (a) place thumb gently on the tip of your shoulderblades; (b) keeping your shoulderblades still and making sure they do not move, lift your other arm to horizontal position. Repeat five times.

'If in doubt, breathe out — and don't forget to stretch out.'

NERVE STRETCHES FOR THE UPPER LIMBS

Median nerve stretch. Hold stretch 20–30 seconds. Repeat three times.

Ulna nerve stretch. Hold stretch 20–30 seconds. Repeat three times a day.

Radial nerve stretch. Hold stretch 20–30 seconds. Repeat three times a day.

CASE HISTORY

Sandi, aged twenty-eight, is a secretary in a top law firm. She presented complaining of shortness of breath, inability to get a breath, and generalised muscular aches and pains, particularly in both forearms and hands.

Over a six-week period during the 1998 Central Business District power blackout in Auckland she had experienced a change in work environment and increased hours of work. Her workload was further increased with the absence of one staff member. On top of this she was moving house, her mother was ill, and she had recently separated from her partner — quite a load!

Sandi, being a very dedicated and hard-working employee, battled on. She ignored warning signs such as headaches, sleep disturbance and the odd ache and pain in her neck and shoulders. To make matters worse, she had stopped taking breaks at work and was not eating regularly. In Sandi's words she was 'too busy'.

Sandi quickly reached the point of exhaustion. Her breathing pattern had altered to an upper chest, rapid, irregular pattern. The adrenaline this produced enabled her to keep going for a short time but eventually her system became overloaded. The alteration in Sandi's breathing pattern was a serious warning sign that recovery was essential. She was rapidly going over the top of the human performance curve to the point where demand was greater than supply.

Sandi finally went to her GP because of her inability to get a decent breath (she thought she might be developing asthma) and because the increasing pain in her arms was interfering with her work. Her GP referred her to me for assessment and treatment of her breathing disorder.

It was not difficult to see that Sandi had gone 'over the top' into exhaustion. Fortunately, it had only been for a period of six weeks. The duration of time spent on the right-hand side of the curve has a bearing on the quantity and quality of time required for recovery.

Sandi's treatment included breathing re-education to effortless breathing (Chapter Five) to return her to the left-hand side of the curve. She took Friday plus the weekend off work to focus on restoring her balance. She was instructed to stop and reinforce the relaxed breathing pattern any time she felt her breathing change. She commented: 'By the end of the weekend I felt light, like a weight had been lifted off my shoulders. I started to feel what it was like to have energy again, plus my sleep wasn't a problem. I used the breathing prior to sleep and went out like a light and felt quite refreshed — something I hadn't felt for a very long time. The pain in my arms decreased significantly.'

Focusing on the breath and applying it to the tasks of everyday life was particularly important for Sandi to improve her awareness, especially while typing, as she was falling into the trap of breath holding. We made it a priority for Sandi to have breaks and, recognising that she became so focused on her work that she would often forget, she initially used a timer every five minutes. This was the cue to stop, pause, breathe out, take a low, slow breath in through the nose, pause, then continue.

After about two weeks Sandi began to recognise when she was breath holding and was able to correct herself prior to the prompting of the timer. Sandi also used the agreed method of placing green dots in strategic places at home, for example, on the telephone, fridge and front door, and in her car. These served as a good reminder to stop, breathe out and relax.

The aches and pains in Sandi's arms were typical of the condition called 'OOS' (occupational overuse syndrome) in New Zealand and 'RSI' (repetitive strain injury) in the USA. I have found that all the people I see with this condition have a breathing disorder.

A specific stretching regime was recommended for Sandi's muscles, which had been overworked. She was also given lifestyle advice on general exercise, regular eating and relaxation to ensure quality sleep.

Within three weeks Sandi was feeling great and all signs and symptoms had disappeared. She is now well equipped for the future to prevent toppling over again.

Sandi commented: *'I now realise the importance of the breathing. I just can't believe how something so simple is so powerful. It's amazing — everyone working at computers should be aware of this. I also realise it is something I need to be aware of for the rest of my life.'*

TEN

BREATHE WELL,
SPEAK WELL

The physical apparatus for oral communication includes the larynx, the oropharynx and the nasopharynx (the oral and nasal cavities). The voice is produced by the breath striking the vocal folds (formerly known as cords), which are contained within the larynx. The throat, tongue, lips and soft palate modify the sound. The quality of the voice is also affected by air escaping out the nose, for example, the sound alters when we have a blocked nose.

A disturbance of your breathing pattern could lead to or contribute to a voice problem. Voice portrays emotion and can emphasise different feelings, for example, a word spoken sharply can reflect a different meaning from the same word spoken softly. A mother is soon able to tell whether her baby's cry is of hunger or pain. Before babies are able to form words they must learn to control their breathing.

A common problem in New Zealand is that we speak too rapidly — how often have you been unable to decipher that message or phone number left on the answerphone? With increased speed of speech comes a delivery full of 'gasps' and poor pronunciation; eventually one runs out of air. When people feel nervous their sentences are often full of throat clearing, sniffing or grunting noises.

As a therapist all these sounds have different meanings, for example, speed-gasps and not getting enough air is indicative of a braced diaphragm and tense upper body causing an upper-chest pattern of breathing. Snorting is indicative of someone who is exhausted (bankrupt on the human performance curve). Long sighs and yawning is indicative of fatigue moving towards exhaustion. Quiet speech that fades could suggest diaphragm weakness, often as a result of a slouched, caving-in posture.

Breathing with your diaphragm is one of the most important tools in controlling the voice. This is an important skill for those who use their voice in their profession, for example, singers, actors, public figures, barristers and television presenters.

Stress plays a large role in our breathing control and therefore on our voice. If we tense the muscles in the neck, the throat and shoulder region become rigid — this alters the delivery of the breath and therefore the voice. Always breathe in through the nose and avoid raising the shoulders or stiffening the muscles in the neck, throat and shoulders. Awareness of effective, effortless breathing helps anxiety and allows a more controlled and confident delivery of voice. Practising quick, calming breaths prior to a presentation will also reduce performance anxiety (see page 120).

TIPS FOR GOOD VOICE CONTROL

1   The nose must be clear.

2   Breathe correctly through the nose.

3   Practise breathing low into the abdomen (diaphragm breathing).

4   Do not raise the shoulders or stiffen the muscles in the neck or throat.

5   Practise in front of a mirror, watching the way you breathe. Keep your head high and shoulders relaxed and breathe through the nose (low and slow).

6   Use punctuation pauses (breathe out).

7   Speak clearly, fluently and with expression.

8   Practise reading aloud.

CASE HISTORY

Mark, aged thirty-five, is a barrister who presented with the problem of 'running out of air' and being unable to get a 'good' breath when talking. On one occasion in the courtroom the judge commented on Mark's lack of expression and the low volume of his voice. This caused Mark anxiety as he had no idea of how to improve his voice and he had not actually realised that he had a problem. With time the anxiety increased to the point where Mark just couldn't face the courtroom. He began to feel palpitations and to break out in a sweat before even entering the court-room. His performance became seriously affected with the avoidance of court work — a difficult pill to swallow for an exceptionally high achiever — and as a result he suffered from severe generalised anxiety.

Mark had no idea why he should experience a voice problem. Examination revealed that he braced his abdomen during breathing and that his pattern was one of upper chest with large hyperinflated breaths — a pattern he thinks he adopted in part because of vanity and a mistaken belief that breathing should be into the upper chest. Mark also divulged that in order not to show any reaction or emotion in court he held himself rigid, which would further contribute to the ineffective use of his voice.

Mark's problems were:

1 **Breathing disorder**: Mark was using the upper chest instead of the lower abdomen.

Treatment: Mark was taught effective breathing (see pages 61–62) and breathing techniques to reduce performance anxiety (see page 112). This enabled him to control sensations of anxiety and as a result his voice control improved.

2 **Posture**: Holding himself rigid caused the diaphragm and thoracic cage to brace. This exacerbated the shallow, upper chest breathing pattern. At each pause in speech Mark would take in air to a point where no more could be inhaled and the voice would fade and control become impossible.

Treatment: Mark was taught to relax his upper body muscles and to 'let go' of the abdomen — a task he found difficult but eventually managed. He did notice that his girth increased in size but dismissed this as *he felt so much better. (See rigid/statue breathing pattern, page 70.)*

3 Muscle imbalance: *Even though Mark attended the gym regularly he spent many hours hunched over a desk. This, together with an incorrect breathing pattern, had led to some muscles becoming stronger and others becoming weaker. His tight anterior chest muscles (pectoralis, upper trapezius and levator scapulae) were caused by his forward body position and the use of these muscles instead of the diaphragm for breathing. The rhomboid and abdominal muscles were considerably weaker.*

Treatment: *A stretching and strengthening programme was initiated. (See stretches on pages 63–65.)*

4 Speed of speech.

Treatment: *Mark was shown the importance of using pauses at commas and fullstops with emphasis on exhalation.*

5 Speaking in court.

Treatment: *Calming breaths before entering court. Mark was taught to centre himself with his breathing prior to speaking by using low, slow abdominal breathing to help relaxation and prevent performance anxiety. He was advised to use well-defined sentences, pausing and expelling air appropriately.*

In summary, the following will assist with good voice production:

BREATHE WELL, SPEAK WELL

● Use effortless breathing (see Chapter Five).

● Make sure you have good posture (see page 58).

● Use short, concise sentences with pauses at punctuation.

● Avoid talking continuously in a long sentence and then taking a sudden inhalation before setting off again. (Practise breathing out and pausing at the end of sentences instead of gasping for air.)

● Practise counting aloud, relatively slowly, up to ten or more as you breathe out. If you cannot reach ten, don't force it, as tensing and preparing for that needed breath will only make your voice worse.

● Visit a speech therapist.

● Remain relaxed and enjoy your voice.

SINGING

Diaphragm breathing is a prerequisite when learning to sing, as this gives control of the voice and assists with performance. Both relaxation and voice control are essential for good performance. If you tense, you will constrict the body, and this can strangle the voice. Singing opera demands a very powerful voice and precise control of breathing. These skills take years of training and practise.

Singing exercises are an excellent way to strengthen the diaphragm. Try singing the following:

You are my sunshine, my only sunshine ... *(BREATHE IN — stomach out)*

You make me happy when skies are grey . . .
(BREATHE IN — stomach out)

You will notice that at first the note will sound loud and strong and as you run out of breath it will become weak and wobbly. When someone is singing it is very obvious whether the diaphragm is being used or not. Posture and in particular head position are also important. If you look down you will constrict your throat. Looking at the level of the ceiling with the head high stops the larynx from closing off. Pitch requires endurance of the voice and for this you must practise using the diaphragm to achieve good control. So keep singing and keep the diaphragm strong.

ELEVEN

BREATHING TO
BEAT STRESS

It is usual to alter your breathing in response to tension or stress. When you begin to overbreathe, the drop in carbon dioxide causes the nervous system to switch on (see Chapter Four). It is often the resulting uncomfortable feelings that you then react to. Just thinking about a situation that has made you feel uncomfortable in the past can stimulate a change in breathing pattern. In order to break the cycle you need to become aware of your breathing. When you are next in a situation that makes you feel nervous, for example, while waiting in the dental surgery or for a job interview or taking that flight, check your breathing pattern and ask yourself the following questions:

● Am I breathing too much air? (Decrease your volume.)

● Am I breathing too fast? (Slow your rate.)

● Am I breath holding? (Keep your rhythm constant.)

Try to identify initiating factors:

● Are you holding in your stomach?

BREATHING TO BEAT STRESS

● Are you talking too fast?

● Have you been rushing? Impatience is often a sign of anxiety.

● Have you increased your use of stimulants, for example, caffeine, alcohol, tobacco or sugar?

ANXIETY

Our breathing changes as we anticipate something that we know makes us feel uncomfortable. We start to breathe faster and deeper into the upper chest, and with time a vicious cycle as seen below is set up and we spiral into what is known as a panic or anxiety attack.

PANIC ATTACKS

It is not uncommon for the memory of an initial panic attack to set up a vicious cycle.

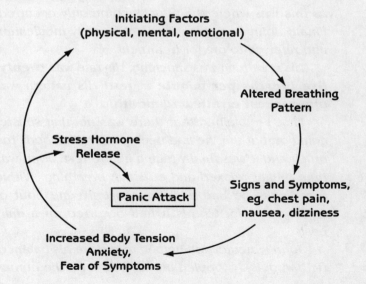

Initiating Factors
(physical, mental, emotional)

Altered Breathing Pattern

Stress Hormone Release

Panic Attack

Signs and Symptoms, eg, chest pain, nausea, dizziness

Increased Body Tension Anxiety, Fear of Symptoms

CASE HISTORY

John, aged twenty-six, works as a chef. He finishes work late and when he presented was averaging only four hours' sleep a night. He had a poor diet and did no exercise. With time this caught up with him and he distinctly remembers his first panic attack.

It was 9 am and he was having coffee with a friend. Out of the blue he started to feel strange, his heart began pounding, pins and needles started down his arms and he couldn't breathe. His friend rushed him to A & E.

All tests showed normal results. John was a little disturbed by this as he found that the feelings were starting to come more often. Each time he panicked and felt he couldn't control the feelings.

Over the next couple of months his problem escalated to a point where he stopped going to cafés, as this was where the attacks commonly occurred. Finally John was prescribed anti-anxiety medication and referred to me for treatment.

*His breathing was shocking. His rate was **twenty-five breaths per minute** at rest! His pattern was **upper chest erratic and mouth**.*

First I explained that there was nothing sinister going on but that he had been pushing his body too much and it was finally telling him to rest. John was then taught relaxed and effective breathing. Within two weeks he had experienced only one bout of anxiety — prior to this it had occurred on a daily basis.

John's medication helped to restore his balance. He had quickly toppled into ill health on the human performance curve and this had manifest as an anxiety disorder. Six months down the track John no longer required medication. He now sees his feelings of anxiety as a friend rather than a foe, as it is telling him to restore some balance into his hectic lifestyle. John says, 'The breathing is a lifesaver. When I start to feel a bit anxious I stop, breathe and relax and it usually passes. If it does not, that's when I know I probably need to eat or sleep more.'

FLYING

Travel is usually associated with a mad rush. Flights are often either first thing in the morning or last thing at night, so people often delay eating until they are on the plane. Last-minute organisation and farewells can involve a lot of rapid talking. Prior even to boarding the plane your breathing rate and pattern will be elevated as a consequence of all these factors. This in turn will stimulate the nervous system and can set in motion the vicious cycle mentioned on page 147. You may not be able to avoid these feelings but you can control them.

Next time you fly, use your breathing to sedate yourself and calm your nerves.

● Slow down your walking and your talking.

● Ensure you are organised.

● Avoid coffee, sugar and chocolate. Eat carbohydrate such as pasta as this elevates the serotonin levels in your brain, making you feel more calm.

● As soon as you are seated check for tension. Drop your shoulders and relax your jaw.

● Focus on your breathing: Low, slow and through the nose. You may find that you have been using your mouth to breathe in large volumes of air. Step down your breathing: From inhaling and exhaling through the mouth to breathing in through the nose and out through the mouth and finally in through the nose and out through the nose. Think 'Let go' and 'I am in control — I have a coping technique' as you breathe out.

● Place your hand on your abdomen to feel your breathing and ensure that it is regular and rhythmical.

● Slow your breathing rate as much as possible.

Remember that often it is the feelings you are panicking about and not the situation. These feelings are just an exaggeration of normal bodily function. They are simply unpleasant and will not harm you.
   The following are also useful whenever you feel anxiety or panic.

● Avoid taking deep breaths — this will only worsen the situation. Try about three short breaths out through pursed lips, swallow, then breathe in through the nose. Repeat.

● 'Grounding' can be helpful. Place your feet on the ground and focus on your feet, including your toes and heels. Imagine that you are breathing out through your feet.

● Count to four breathing out and then hold your breath for a count of four and in for a count of three — a prolonged expiration and pause causes decreased cerebral and physical activity.

BREATHING TO BEAT STRESS

● Symptoms of a panic attack can be reduced by exerting pressure on the breastbone (sternum) with the hand and gently massaging it. This stimulates the baroreceptors and lowers the heart rate.

● If panic persists, as a last resort breathe into cupped hands or a paper bag. This allows you to re-breathe the exhaled carbon dioxide and increase the level in your blood in order to stop further activation of the nervous system. Once under control remove the paper bag and continue relaxed breathing.

Some people find that when they try to slow their breathing the anxiety sensations increase or their signs and symptoms may re-occur. This is common in people who have been bad breathers for a long time. The body has become accustomed to 'running on adrenaline' and reacts when you begin to change it. The main thing is to take your time, and to work on slowing down the rate and reducing the volume of air you are breathing.

SUBSTANCE ABUSE

Substance abuse in today's society is reaching epidemic proportions. The drugs used usually fall into two categories: stimulants and sedatives. Stimulants include caffeine, nicotine, alcohol, cocaine and ecstasy; sedatives include valium and heroin. Both categories are used as a coping mechanism for stress.

Upon removal of any of the above substances a reaction usually occurs, sending the autonomic nervous system into a spin. This withdrawal creates problems in itself, for example, panic attacks, headaches, muscular aches and pains, etc. Breathing is an excellent tool in

the management of these symptoms and in the maintenance of a drug-free lifestyle. (See relaxed breathing,
pages 52–57.)

TWELVE

WOMEN'S HEALTH

PREGNANCY

It is not uncommon for pregnant women to experience shortness of breath, particularly during the final months. As the pregnancy progresses, the angle of the lower rib cage increases, displacing the rib cage outwards. Breathing tends to become more abdominal but the diaphragm has to move further, making it harder work. In addition, the level of the hormone progesterone is raised during pregnancy and this decreases the carbon dioxide sensitivity in the respiratory centre. The lowered carbon dioxide level can lead to an increase in ventilation — as much as fifty per cent more than usual. Relaxed breathing will help to counteract the hormonal effect and prevent over-breathing.

BREATHING DURING LABOUR

Many women attending ante-natal classes will quiz the teacher on how to breathe during labour. The most important thing is calm, easy breathing. Relaxed breathing helps to maintain a good blood flow to the uterus, which is beneficial to both the mother and the baby. It also stimulates the parasympathetic branch of the autonomic nervous system, releasing hormones into the body that will help you relax the uterus and stay calm. Relaxation is the key in maintaining control during labour and birth.

Remember the different types of breathing used by a sprinter and a jogger — one is for speed and the other is for endurance. Calm, easy breathing works to ensure endurance. Think of your labour as a long-distance run — you must pace yourself to prevent fatigue setting in too early. Breathing like a sprinter will lead to exhaustion and to stress for both you and your baby.

Relaxed Breathing

1   In sitting position place one hand on your chest and the other on your abdomen. Focus on your breathing. Feel the movement and the pattern, and think about it for a few minutes.

2   Breathe all the air out through your nose or mouth and relax. Think about letting your stomach rise as you breathe in, feeling the air move your lower hand.

3   Feel your stomach and lower hand drop as you breathe out.

4   Try a gentle pause at the end of the breath out.

5   If this is difficult try breathing in a little lower to the bottom of your lungs.

6   Continue with this pattern aiming for a smooth, regular, rhythmical pattern.

7   Remember do **not** breathe large volumes.

In Different Labour Positions

● Try using relaxed breathing on all fours so that you can rock gently to your breathing pattern. *Remember:* Low and slow through the nose; focus on the breath out. Breathe in and rock forward, breathe out and rock back.

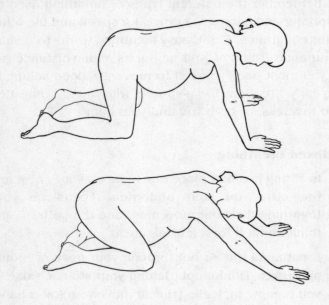

● Try standing supported by the wall – breathe in and rock up, breathe out and rock down.

Increased Strength of Contractions

Breathe in, breathe out and let go . . . If contractions are strong, purse your lips (as if to whistle) and blow when you breathe out. Try to exhale as much air as possible. Breathe in through your nose and repeat.

As contractions become stronger the urge is often to breathe in a deep, rapid manner. This can lead to hyperventilation leaving you dizzy and short of breath. The main focus is to ensure that all the air is expelled. Remember, 'If in doubt, breathe out.'

During very strong contractions, especially when you have been instructed not to push, you can focus on three or four blowing breaths out. Pause, breathe in through the nose in stepped fashion so that it is not too deep, then blow out again with pursed lips: Blow . . . blow . . . blowww . . .

MOTHERHOOD

Women nowadays spend far less time in hospital following childbirth. The average stay is two to three days compared to ten days fifteen to twenty years ago. This suits some mothers but it is generally felt that many are leaving ill-equipped and still physically tired.

Breast-feeding is often an issue that if not resolved during the brief hospital stay or the few follow-up visits from a midwife can leave the mother struggling. Feelings of guilt, concern and anxiety may be experienced, and this can have a spiralling effect. Relaxed breathing will help with milk production and flow. The baby will feel your relaxed, rhythmical pattern and in turn feel more relaxed. It is also important that your baby is a nose breather. This is a prerequisite to 'good' feeding.

The average age for first-time mothers is twenty-seven. The trend, especially among professional women, is to have children at a later age. This brings a host of problems, not least the enormous change in lifestyle. Professional women who have been accustomed to having control in their lives are suddenly faced with a baby who does not work like clockwork.

Then comes the juggling act of children, partner, work and running a household. Working mothers with these multiple roles often admit that it is exhausting. As funding to support groups such as Plunket and family centres decreases, the mother of today needs to become more equipped to endure the stresses and strains.

Breathing is a wonderful tool to help calm in times of turbulence. As one mother commented: *'The amazing thing I noticed with my breathing was that when I used it to calm myself the children relaxed as well — I felt like I had some control.'*

MENSTRUATION AND PMT

Research has shown that as progesterone levels within the body are raised prior to menstruation it can induce a state called 'respiratory alkalosis' where there is a decrease in the blood levels of carbon dioxide. As we have seen, this can lead to over-breathing and symptoms of hyperventilation, adding to premenstrual problems.

Many of my patients comment that when they have learned to breathe correctly they notice an improvement in their symptoms of PMT.

It has been shown that certain contraceptive pills enhance the effect of progesterone on respiration. It has been suggested that those containing norethindrone and mestranol or ethinyl estradiol can cause hyper-ventilatory changes.

MENOPAUSE

Freedman and Woodward in an article, 'Behavioural Treatment of Menopausal Hot Flushes', have reported that using simple breathing procedures results in a significant reduction in menopausal hot flushes. They see regular relaxed breathing as useful for women with hot flushes who are unable to receive hormone replacement therapy or who do not wish to take it.

CASE HISTORY

Helen, aged forty-nine, real estate agent, presented with a host of signs and symptoms including flushing and the anxiety associated with it. Within one month of breathing exercises Helen had noticed the flushes had disappeared completely. She was also sleeping much better, her confidence had returned and she was able to venture out and cope in public places. Helen still practises her breathing every night without fail because of the changes she has experienced. She intends to make this a life-long practice.

INCONTINENCE

Relaxed breathing can be extremely useful for urge incontinence in helping to dissipate the urge. A major problem with urge incontinence is the anxiety when in public. Where is the closest toilet? What if I cough too hard? Will I make it home? I can't wait in this long queue! The natural response is to tense up. Unfortunately, this tension serves as a signal to the nervous system to speed up, increasing bladder contraction and the urge to go to the toilet. The more relaxed you can be in such situations the better.

1   Breathe in through the nose using low, slow breaths and as you breathe out let go of all the body's tension.

2   When the body is relaxed you must learn to hold only the pelvic floor tight. This is no easy task but it is all a matter of co-ordination — a little like rubbing your stomach in circles and patting your head at the same time. It involves breathing out and letting the body tension go while at the *same time* pulling up your pelvic floor. A lot of practice may be needed but it will pay off.

3   Using the **green dot method**, place dots around the house — on the fridge, telephone and in the car — and every time you see these dots, stop, breathe out and let the body relax whilst gently holding up the pelvic floor.

If you find that this is too difficult, talk to your GP about seeing a physiotherapist who specialises in women's health. Focusing on your breathing when you feel the urge to pass urine will help to calm the system to allow you plenty of time to get to the bathroom.

GYNAECOLOGICAL EXAMINATIONS

Smear tests and other gynaecological examinations are not pleasant but are a necessity for preventative health care. Relaxed breathing will assist in relaxing the uterus so that the procedure is as comfortable as possible.

THIRTEEN

ASTHMA

In New Zealand fifteen per cent of the population (about 450,000 people) have been told by a doctor that they have asthma. In Australia thirty per cent of the population will have a respiratory disorder that is consistent with asthma at some time in their lives.

Asthma is a condition that occurs in people with hyperactive air passages. It is characterised by a narrowing of the airways. The bronchi consist of three layers:

1   An outer layer of incomplete rings of cartilage. This makes the bronchus stiff so as to maintain its shape.

2   A middle circular layer of smooth muscle which alters the size of the bronchus by contracting and relaxing.

3   An inner mucosal lining which consists of mucus, mucus-producing glands and little hairs called cilia.

When a person experiences an asthma attack, the following occurs:

ASTHMA

1   The smooth muscle spasms, narrowing the airway.

2   The mucosal lining swells, further narrowing the airway.

3   Excess mucus is produced, which blocks the airway even more.

4   The upper chest muscles start to take over breathing (it is not uncommon to experience pain in these muscles following an attack). Asthmatics often use the upper chest muscles as a normal pattern of breathing and this can lead to a sore neck and shoulder muscles, upper back problems and headaches.

Clearly the above combination will make it very difficult to breathe. Asthma may be triggered by exposure to one or more of a large range of stimuli such as exertion, emotion (stress), dust mites, pollen, animal dander, changes in temperature, viruses and, less commonly, food allergies. If you suspect a particular allergen such as pollen or a specific food it is important to have a sensitivity test as you may be able to be desensitised.

The exact cause of asthma is still unclear and numerous studies are currently being conducted. Research suggests that if allergens to which a mother is particularly sensitive are avoided during pregnancy it will minimise the chances of her child developing asthma. Asthma Auckland is currently launching a campaign aimed at educating expectant mothers.

Certain factors are helpful if you have asthma:

1   It is imperative to discuss your medication with your GP so that you fully understand how it acts and know

what to do if your asthma worsens.

2   Your environment may need to be modified. The bedroom in particular may need to be cleaned thoroughly, carpets cleaned often, and soft toys washed in hot soapy water and then frozen at least once a fortnight. These measures are an attempt to keep dust mites to a minimum. Cats can be a nightmare for asthmatics. Diana Hart of Asthma Auckland comments that the safest pet for an asthmatic is a goldfish.

3   Avoid smoke.

4   Minimise stress.

5   Learn to breathe well through the nose and take care of the health of your nose (see pages 33–36).

6   Learn to breathe with a 'good' pattern (see Chapter Five).

Bad breathing also increases the level of histamine in the body, which can increase sensitivity to trigger factors. Correct breathing will assist with desensitising the body.

CASE HISTORY

Teresa, aged thirty-two, has suffered from asthma all her life. After a series of infections and general ill health she felt it was time for action. When she presented to me one year ago she was quite unwell. It was common for her to experience three to four chest infections a year.

Teresa had always been an upper chest, mouth

breather. She was taking a couple of puffs of her reliever a day and two puffs of a preventor night and morning. She couldn't exercise without using her reliever several times throughout the session.

Initially, Teresa was taught to nose breathe. This took a few months to master, although she started to notice changes after just a few weeks. She found it very difficult at first and felt quite discouraged as her nose had been so congested that she felt she couldn't inhale sufficient air. However, she persevered and now has very little congestion in her nose, and breathing through the nose feels natural to her.

Teresa was instructed in relaxed breathing using the diaphragm. This also felt very strange to her and it was several months before it felt natural. On bad days she would lie down and concentrate on her breathing to get back into the routine of breathing correctly.

Teresa's triggers are stress, exercise and different environments, for example, dusty or smoky rooms. She is now fully aware of the way she breathes and if she begins to feel short of breath and tight in the chest, her first step now is not to reach for her reliever but to try and control the feelings with her breathing. She focuses on low, slow nose breathing until all her signs and symptoms disappear — this happens most of the time but she knows to use her reliever medication if she still has signs and symptoms.

Teresa has not had any infections this year and is feeling strong. She has two puffs of her preventor

*a day and only uses her reliever prior to high-impact
exercise. In her words: 'Learning to breathe properly
has changed my entire life. I have heaps more
energy, I need less sleep and generally feel like a
new, healthier, calmer person. When I first visited
Tania I thought that learning to breathe correctly was
an insurmountable task. A year later I can honestly
say that it wasn't as hard as I'd expected and it has
certainly been worth the effort.'*

Asthma can affect anyone — there is no difference in
incidence across socio-economic groups as once thought.
However, statistics show that in lower socio-economic
groups the severity is worse, probably because of
problems of overcrowding, difficulty in controlling the
environment and the cost of visiting a GP. (Many people
are still unaware that there is no charge for children under
the age of five years to see a GP.)

EXERCISES FOR ASTHMA SUFFERERS
Asthma sufferers often breathe using large hyper-
inflatory breaths. This means that they take a breath
when there is still air remaining in the lungs, so they
begin to 'puff up' the lungs. This further triggers airway
sensitivity. Research has shown that it is vital to
decrease this retention of air in the lungs.

The longer someone breathes like this the more
accustomed the lungs become to the increase in air and
it may take weeks or perhaps months to reverse the
process. It is important to begin exhaling against
increased resistance.

Try this:

● With your lips pursed as if whistling, blow out as much air as possible. Now breathe in through the nose and again blow out as much air as possible through your pursed lips. Pause for a second at the end of the out breath. You may wish to try blowing out through a straw. If you practise this exercise frequently (I recommend once hourly) your lungs will become accustomed to less air. Most of us need prompting so use the **green dot method** of placing dots in strategic places (on the fridge, phone, mirror, in the car, etc) and each time you see the dot blow out as much air as possible, pause, breathe in then continue your activity.

Note that this exercise is only effective for those who hyper-inflate or mouth breathe. If you find that you are unable to alter this pattern yourself I recommend that you discuss this with your GP who can refer you for assessment and treatment by a health professional with expertise in this area.

I also recommend that you practise relaxed breathing twice a day (see page 52). If you cannot get the air out and experience too much air hunger, use the resistance of pursed lips until your body allows the nose to take over.

I firmly believe that the second most important thing to medication is the breathing pattern. Remember: If in doubt, breathe out.

1 Several patients have commented on the benefit of initially assisting the air out by placing your hand on your upper chest and as you breathe out pulling your sternum bone down.

2 Alternatively, in sitting position place your hands on

your lower back and try to bring your elbows together. A friend or family member can assist by pulling your elbows towards each other. This encourages expansion of the chest.

3   Lifting both arms above your head also assists with diaphragmatic breathing.

4   A mobile rib cage and relaxed muscles are important for effective breathing. Try the exercises on pages 72–75.

Getting down on the ground on all fours and relaxing the stomach will introduce you to what it feels like to breathe abdominally. In this position it is virtually impossible not to breathe using the abdomen.

EXERCISES FOR CHILDREN

It is important to set aside a regular time for children to practise good breathing. I suggest twice a day until they begin to breathe automatically through the nose — low and slow at rest. Lie or sit with them and practise relaxed breathing together — it is good for you as well.

Games can be used for younger children:

●   Practise blowing a candle so that the flame does not go out. Make sure the breath out is low and slow, and then use the nose to breathe in towards the stomach.

●   Blow up balloons. Ensure that all the air is blown out and make sure that the breath in is through the nose and down towards the abdomen.

●   Blow a small ball across the table in a controlled pattern. See who can blow it in a straight line. Try blowing with a straw to increase resistance.

Make up a story or a game to go with the following exercise:

1   Breathe in . . . and in . . . and stretch all the way up to the ceiling. Now blow out and drop down to the floor.

2   Standing up and keeping your lower body still, move forward then backward. Breathe in as you move forward and out as you move backward. Make a 'haaaa' sound with each breath out. This relaxes the tongue and jaw, opening the chest and relaxing the diaphragm.

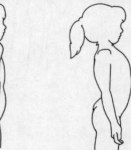

3   Bending forward, move your arms from side to side as if swinging a golf club. Breathe in as you swing to the right and out as you swing to the left.

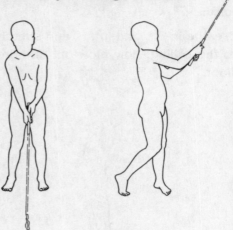

4   In sitting position, breathe in, lean forward and breathe out. Purse your lips as you do so and blow out-out-out. Repeat three times.

5   Lying over a pillow under your upper chest to open
    this region, breathe in and lift arms up and over your
    head, and out back down by your sides.

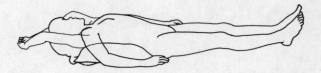

   These exercises help to strengthen the diaphragm
and encourage the use of the nose. Stronger muscles
will lead to less fatigue.

FOURTEEN

JOAN – A SPECIAL CASE HISTORY

J oan is a 67-year-old tutor in fashion and apparel. She has had a lifelong history of ill health, presenting with extreme fatigue, inability to get a 'good breath', tingling and numbness in hands and feet, chest tightness, inability to get to sleep, poor sleep, waking unrefreshed, muscle aches and pains in neck and back, nausea, dizziness and anxiety.

When I first saw Joan, her breathing rate was twenty-two breaths per minute, her breathing pattern was erratic with upper chest and mouth moving large volumes of air. Her speech was interspersed with gasps and sighs, and no punctuation. Her body awareness and posture were poor and very rigid. Upon analysis it was concluded Joan had an extremely disordered breathing pattern. Treatment involved breathing re-evaluation. After three treatments Joan's breathing rate was thirteen breaths per minute with a rhythmical, regular, nose, and lower abdominal pattern. Her speech is now slower and well punctuated, her posture relaxed and 'good'.

Tania: What do you think the breathing awareness has done for you?

Joan: First of all it made me very angry to think that I could have been using it for twenty years. After I got over being angry, I couldn't believe that such a simple thing could help me. You have no idea what I have been through over the years and how this has affected my life.

Tania: What are the changes you have noticed over the last week?

Joan: I now think about things before I do them. I used to rush in like a lunatic and do everything quickly. I feel much more relaxed, especially driving. Before I came to see you I used to get so uptight if someone got close up behind me — I'd nearly have a fit. Now they can sit there and it doesn't worry me. Driving now is just great.

. I can feel my fingers now — on the third or fourth day I lost the puffiness in them. My legs aren't so stiff — it's still there but not as bad and I can sit for longer. The swelling in my legs has gone down quite a bit too. My muscles only ache when I get excited and am not breathing properly. It's absolutely amazing — I wouldn't have believed it.

My relationship with my husband is much better. We were on the verge of separating. He keeps saying, 'You're looking better, you're acting better, you're talking slower, and you are seeing things differently. It's almost like you have been in a haze for twenty years.'

Last week I woke with a heavy chest pain and thought it was a heart attack. When I got up I felt dizzy and felt like I was almost not in control of myself. This week there is no problem. I have hardly any palpitations and only get chest pain and tightness when I am not breathing properly.

It's like you're desperately trying to hold on to some control of your life and you don't know what's causing you to do things. I used to go home, have tea and flop on the bed exhausted. I must have been a bad breather all my life. I am convinced there has not been enough research done on the topic.

My boss can't believe the change either. He thinks I'm so relaxed now. I am saying the same things only differently and more calmly. Until last Wednesday, when I answered the phone people would ask if I had been running as I was so short of breath. My daughter said the other night that I was not huffing and puffing as if I had been running.

And I'm eating differently. Once upon a time I used to eat a meal and not remember eating it, not only because of the speed of eating it but also because I used to feel so spaced out. I'm not eating so fast now so I'm not swallowing as quickly. Before I used to choke as I wasn't getting my breath properly. Now I breathe in between mouthfuls. Last week I was hardly eating at all as I was so scared I would choke. The nausea is all gone now too.

I've felt tired for about twenty years but it's been chronic for the last three years. I used to get up, have a wash and think that was as far as I could go. I'd have to force myself to do things.

My sleep has improved but it's still not fantastic. I still yawn a couple of times a day but before I was doing it perpetually.

Joan's daughter, Gloria, takes over:

For as far back as I can remember Mum has felt tired and worn out. In the weekends she would lie down after lunch and then in the evening after dinner she would lie down again because she felt exhausted. This was her pattern for many years. Yet all her life she has held down a full-time job and at sixty-seven is still working full time, which is to be admired.

Mum would worry about the least little thing and get very uptight. I live in Wanganui and when we went up to Auckland for holidays when the children were young they would want to go to the zoo and the beach and on picnics. Mum would always find a nice shady spot under a tree and curl up. When one of the children asked where Nana was the reply would always be 'resting under the tree'.

I used to get frustrated because if I told Mum something I would have to repeat it about six times. She would ask me a question and I would think, 'I've already told you that about five times,' rolling my eyes as I said it. I would always wonder why she never listened. I would feel hurt and think she was not interested. But I accepted this as being my mother and I love her dearly. We have been through a lot over the years and she is my best friend. She is always there to talk to even if sometimes she didn't listen.

Mum has diabetes and in March 1997 her doctor decided to put her on insulin in the evenings and keep her on tablets during the day. Mum did not like the idea of having to inject herself but she overcame that hurdle. In December the doctor decided that she should use insulin all the time. It was at this time that things got worse. She developed an awful cough and even with antibiotics she couldn't shake it for nearly six months. April arrived and Mum had been going to the doctor nearly every week and sometimes twice a week. She had a total of twenty-eight blood tests from February to May. I was ringing every night because I was so worried. She would get breathless talking on the phone, yawn and drift off into her own little world. I would feel like I was talking to myself.

Towards the end of April Mum was taken to hospital by ambulance and placed on oxygen for about five hours. She was given X-rays and told that she had a shadow on each lung in the same spot — cancer! I was really upset and cried buckets. My partner had been a medic in the Navy and told me that a shadow on each lung in the same place was highly unlikely to be cancer and more likely to be a virus. But I still worried. On the Friday evening I rang to see how she was and found that she had discharged herself.

The following week Mum was told that she had pneumonia and was referred by her GP to a lung specialist.

I decided to surprise her with a visit. On Saturday morning we went to the hairdressers, which wore her out. As we were leaving she felt dizzy and faint. Later I remember feeling angry as I was getting the dinner ready. How could her doctor let her get so bad?

Driving home to Wanganui I was feeling very worried but hopeful that her visit to the lung specialist would be fruitful. I telephoned the evening after her appointment and asked how she had got on. The doctor had asked a lot of questions about all her ailments and had then told her that she had 'hyperventilation syndrome', a breathing pattern disorder. I think Mum had felt that her time was approaching to meet her maker and when she was told what was wrong with her I guess she felt as if she had won Lotto.

Mum was then referred to Tania, who went through her notes and instructed her on treatment. No pills! Just the green dots for reminders and ten minutes of correct breathing morning and night — breathing through the nose down to the waist, twelve breaths a minute. It sounds hard to believe it is so simple.

It has been four weeks since Mum started the breathing exercises. I phone every night and I have noticed a difference in her voice. She is not getting puffed or yawning . . . and she's listening! Speaking to her recently she let out this lovely laugh, which is something I have never heard from her before. She is not uptight.

I'm finding it hard to believe that something so simple as breathing was her problem. My friends know that Mum's not well and now when they ask how she is I say, 'She is really good and getting better *every day.' When I tell them that her problem was that she was not breathing correctly they look at me as if I am half-witted, but had I not seen it with my own eyes I would also have found it hard to believe.*

Mum will still have her bad days with her diabetes but she is on the right track.

In Summary:

BREATHING is the body's best-kept secret.

RHYTHM for relaxation and recovery. Find your pattern, learn what gives you instant calm and focus on this several times a day.

ENERGY for endurance. Know your energy levels and when you are spending too much. Recognise the breathing pattern associated with your different energy levels.

AWARENESS of your warning signs. Listen to your body and teach your children awareness at an early age.

TASK specific. Fit the breath to the task. Don't breathe like a sprinter when you are jogging, don't breathe like a jogger when you are resting.

HEALTH: Breathing well is essential for wellness and vitality.

EXPIRE: 'If in doubt, breathe out.'

BIBLIOGRAPHY

Bessel, J. and Gervirtz, R., 'Effects of Breathing Retraining versus Cognitive and Somatic Components of State Anxiety and on Performance of Female Gymnasts', *California School of Professional Psychology*, San Diego, California, 1997.

Bradley, Dinah, *Hyperventilation Syndrome*, Tandem Press, New Zealand, 1991.

Caudron, Shari, 'The Wellness Payoff', *CO Personnel Journal*, Denver, July 1990.

Cottle, M.H., 'The Work, Ways, Positions and Patterns of Nasal Breathing (Relevance in Heart and Lung Illness)', *Proceedings of the American Rhinologic Society*, 1972.

Davis, Martha; Robbin Eikelman, Elizabeth; McKay, Matthew, *The Relaxation and Stress Reduction Workbook*, New Harbinger, 5th Edition, March 1997, Oakland, USA.

Evertt, T., Dennis, M. and Ricketts, E, *Physiotherapy in Mental Health: A Practical Approach*, Butterworth & Heinemann, UK, 1995.

Farhi, Donna, *The Breathing Book*, Simon & Schuster, NSW, Australia, 1997.

Freedman, R. and Woodward, S., 'Behavioural Treatment of Menopausal Hot Flushes', *American Journal of Obstetrics and Gynaecology*, Vol. 167, 1992.

BIBLIOGRAPHY

Gardiner, W.N., 'The Pathophysiology of Hyperventilation Disorder', *Chest*, Vol. 109, February 1997.

Gray, John, *Your Guide To The Alexander Technique*, Victor Gollanz, London, 1990.

Le Merre, 'Pregnancy and the Respiratory Function', *Rev-Mal-Respir*, 1988, Vol. 5 (3), pp. 249–254.

Lum, L.C., 'Breathing exercises in the treatment of hyperventilation and chronic anxiety states', *Chest, Heart and Stroke Journal*, 1977, Vol. 2, pp. 6–11.

Lundberg, J.; Wheitzberg, E.; Nordvall, S.L., et al, 'Primarily Nasal Origin of Exhaled Nitric Oxide and Absence in Kartagener's Syndrome', *European Respiratory Journal*, Vol. 7, 1994, pp. 1501–1504.

Machiad, Niromichi, 'Influences of progesterone on arterial blood and CSF acid-base balance in women', *Journal of Applied Physiology*, Dec. 1981, Vol. 51 (6); pp. 1433, 1436.

Mead, J., 'Volume Displacement Body Plethysmograph for Respiratory Measurements in Human Subjects', *Journal of Applied Physiology*, Vol. 15, 1960, pp. 736–740.

Negas, V., 'Observations on the Exchange of Fluid in the Nose and Respiratory Tract', *Annals of Otology, Rhinology, and Laryngology*, Vol. 66, 1957, pp. 344–363.

Nixon, P.G.F., 'An Appraisal of Thomas Lewis's Effort Syndrome', *Quarterly Journal of Medicine*, Vol. 88, 1995, pp. 741–747.

Nixon, P.G.F., 'Effort Syndrome: Hyperventilation and Reduction of Anaerobic Threshold', *Biofeedback and Self-Regulation*, Vol. 19, No. 2, 1994.

Peper, E.D., et al, 'Repetitive Strain Injury: Electromyography Applications in Physical Therapy', 1994. Correspondence via email.

Peper, E.D., 'Muscle Tension and Subjective Awareness at the Keyboard', SUBJ23 DOC, 1994. Correspondence via email.

Rama, Swami, *Science of Breath*, Himalayan International Institute, 1979.

Rosen, S.D., 'Hyperventilation and the Chronic Fatigue Syndrome', *Quarterly Journal of Medicine,* Vol. 87, 1994, pp. 373–374.

Smith, C.A. and Mines, A.H., 'Ventilatory Response of Humans to Chronic Contraceptive Pill Administration', *Respiration*, Vol. 43, 1982, pp. 179–185.

Timmons, B. and Ley, R., (eds), *Behavioral and Psychological Approaches to Breathing Disorders*, Plenum Press, New York, 1994.

University of Oregon Graduate School of Management, 'Cost–benefit Analysis of the Coors' Wellness Program', University of Oregon, December 1988.

Widmer, S. and Conway, A., et al, 'Hyperventilation: A Correlate and Predictor of Debilitating Performance Anxiety in Musicians', *Med Probl Perform Art*, 1997.

For further information please do not hesitate to contact me at:

BREATHING WORKS
Breathing Pattern Disorders Clinic
1 Maidstone Street,
Ponsonby
Auckland
New Zealand

Phone: 64-09-360 1477
Fax: 64-09-360 8968
e-mail: breathe@ihug.co.nz